Notes from An Underground Restaurant

IMPROVISATIONS THROUGH FOOD AND MUSIC

by Philip Gelb

This book is dedicated to Matthew Sperry, a brilliant creative musician, a voracious eater, a fine cook, and as good a friend as I can ever be blessed to have in my life. Rest In Peace, Matt, your memory will always be savored.

CONTENTS

TEMPEH, TOFU & BEANS

DESSERTS

WHERE AND WHEN DO WE EAT?

Where and when do we eat? This is the primary question for the Deep Listening Band wherever we go to perform. Philip Gelb has a great answer for this question, at least for the twenty lucky people who reserve their places for his dinner concerts. Phil provides superb, beautifully prepared vegetarian food and beautifully curated music performed right at the table in his home.

I met Phil long ago when he was still a student in Florida. He reached out to me to perform some of my music. I was struck then by his sensibility for experimental music and his ability to produce concerts. The high quality of these concerts was shown by his discerning choice of composers.

Later in California we played together with pianist Dana Reason in a trio that we dubbed The Space Between. This title referred partly to our different tunings; I with my accordion in just intonation, Dana with her piano in equal temperament, and Phil with his shakuhachi in shaku perturbation. The space between our different tunings was a richly interesting musical negotiation in our improvisations!

We made a number of recordings with The Space Between, often with luminary guest bass players such as Barre Phillips, Joëlle Léandre, and Matthew Sperry. These players added immensely to our irrational mix of tunings and were able to navigate in and between our spaces.

It was later, after I had left California and The Space Between that I began hearing about Phil's dinner concerts. I found out what a fantastic chef he was when I was invited to perform at one of his dinners. Phil's dinners are artistic masterpieces. From the finest fresh vegetables to be found in the Bay Area he makes visually stunning and marvelously tasty courses.

I didn't have to ask my question (When and where do we eat?) when I performed for the dinner concert. Food and music go well together. The intimacy of dining with the audience and then performing in their midst is especially wonderful and exceptional.

Phil has an informed following that understands the music and the food that is served. Expectations are high for the best of both food and music. Somehow the combination of Phil's remarkable musicianship as a shakuhachi player and improviser, his discernment as a curator of experimental music, and his creativity with food has established a special venue for those who can appreciate the generosity of their accomplished host.

Pauline Oliveros

9/27/2015
Blood Moon

THE SPACE BETWEEN SOUND AND SAVOR

I remember the first time Phil reached out to me in an email and introduced himself. "Hi, I'm a big fan of yours. I'm also a vegan chef and I play the shakuhachi."

It's not every day that someone writes to you and tells you that they play the shakuhachi, especially in the same sentence as being a vegan chef. I mean, how many people even know what it is? I knew then, before I even met him, that he and I would be good friends.

Years ago, during my super soul-searching days of my early twenties, I had dabbled in the shakuhachi myself. I'm pretty sure I was the only woman who ever showed up at my aging sensei's doorstep begging him to teach me; in fact, I may have been the only woman in Japan to hold this enigmatic bamboo flute to my lips. I stress that I merely dabbled, because, while I learned to make something a bit more pleasant than noise, Phil is a master, from whose shakuhachi those mysterious, haunting sounds emanate and carry you away until you find yourself on the set of Rashomon. The first time I heard him really play was during a raucous Thanksgiving dinner where he brought the chatter to utter silence, and a deep, communal meditation followed as our minds slipped away quietly into the richness of his tones.

Japanese music, particularly the shakuhachi, is rich with quarter-tones, those notes between the notes of a Western scale. Some might think that they are just flat or sharp, but they are actually the exploration of the nuances between the notes. Food is like that. You can just play the straight notes, or you can explore between them, and add color and mystery to the flavors. Phil approaches both music and food in the same way. When you bite into one of his dishes and think you have an understanding of it, a little hidden flavor pops up, that flavor between flavors, like notes between notes.

The shakuhachi is a simple-looking instrument that belies its appearance. There are only five holes for your fingers to work with, but an almost infinite variety of sounds are possible, depending on how much of each hole you cover with your fingers. As rustic an instrument as it looks, it requires subtlety in handling and is capable of great sophistication. This, too, is like Phil -- his culinary creations are beautifully rustic and yet layered with a cacophony of flavors. What seems a simple dish -- just greens, or latkes, or a black bean puree -- reveals a colorful landscape that makes you pause, tilt your head as you smile and wonder what that little spice might be, then invites you to explore it further with another mouthful.

There is truth to the sound of the shakuhachi. As textured as the voice of Billie Holiday, as gentle as the sound of rain, as quiet as the whispering wind through the forest, as thunderous as rocks tumbling down the mountainside, it is an instrument capable of all scopes of sound. Crying, wailing, moaning, groaning, raw, yet precise -- just the truth, without the fanfare or pretense. Sitting through one of Phil's underground meals is a similar experience. Pure, simple, honest. You know the care that was taken at every step of the preparation, from the handmade soba noodles, to bagels, to his beloved tempeh -- he doesn't just open up boxes and packages and pretend. Every component is carefully, truthfully crafted, and you taste the depth in every bite.

We need more Phils in the culinary world, people who cook the truth from the bottom up, who aren't trying to impress or show off, but simply want to share their connection with foods that come from the earth, from their hands, from their hearts. I am so glad Philip Gelb has finally penned his life in this beautiful book that sings like his shakuhachi.

Miyoko Schinner

10/13/2015

NOTES FROM AN UNDERGROUND RESTAURANT

When one thinks of gourmet dining and world-renowned musicians, images of the gritty part of industrial West Oakland probably do not come to mind. For the past decade, in a loft space in a former rubber factory, I have been hosting a series of dinner concerts, once or twice a month. Over eighty musicians from various genres and thirteen countries have appeared on the series. The same musicians who perform on luxurious stages around the world, such as Lincoln Center, the Sydney Opera House, and Bimhuis, also appear in this small loft space, performing for twenty highly enthusiastic listeners and diners.

Why underground?

A question that is often asked is why I started an underground series instead of opening a restaurant and performance space. Many reasons! First, of course, is finance. I simply did not have the money to start a restaurant, which is quite expensive. And the risk of a restaurant is huge, with fifty percent failing in the first year in the US and ninety percent in the first five years. Second, when I started this series I was still actively involved playing and teaching music and touring regularly. Opening a "real" restaurant would make teaching and touring prohibitive, which, at the time, I did not want to give up. Third, the idea of TAZ or Temporary Autonomous Zones is of great interest to me. Ever since I was a teen and read George Orwell's *Homage to Catalonia*, about his time spent in the Spanish Civil War, I have identified myself, politically, as an anarchist. TAZ are one way to put anarchist theory into action both physically and economically.

TAZ is the idea of creating temporary structures outside of the ruling forms of control. This was already happening in various places, particularly in some art scenes in Eastern Europe where "underground events" were necessary since certain kinds of performance were considered illegal. A TAZ is creating something in the moment, something that will only happen on that occasion, not to be replayed again. A Temporary Autonomous Zone is a direct response to the corporate-controlled state we exist in; it goes against the grain of the monoculture, providing a different paradigm that is in opposition to global capital and corporate structures. It is a response to totalitarianism and is something that inevitably happens.

TAZ are about community and the development of community. The underground restaurant develops community around two essentials of human existence: food and music (and more recently we have added films to some events). We have to eat in order to survive. Do we have to listen? Do we have to feel the vibrations of music? The simple fact that every known culture has some form of music provides the obvious answer. Food feeds the body, music feeds the spirit. Most of our guests at the underground restaurant sit at communal tables where new friendships and relationships are often created. Couples often come, as well as pairs or groups of friends, but we also have many who come alone, knowing they will see other regulars as well as meet new people and be most welcome.

And food, when seen in the larger picture, should always be about community. Community is developed; some examples: when you meet the farmers who grow your food and the tofu maker or tempeh maker in town who makes your food and the baker at the bakeries who bake your breads. The menus are about community! Always sourced locally (a few obvious exceptions are spices, chocolate, coconuts, and other occasional tropical ingredients) and often from sources we directly know. And, of course, our reputation is to hand make practically everything, right here in our kitchen.

Occasionally bread is sourced from Arizmendi collective in Emeryville, right down the street, or tofu from the two awesome tofu makers in the area, Hodo Soy, which makes yuba and tofu a few blocks away from my kitchen, and Tofu-Yu, which makes exceptional and rare flat tofu in Berkeley. As of recently, a new tempeh maker, Rhizocali, began producing exceptional tempeh a few blocks away in the same neighborhood of West Oakland! Befriending the two women behind the business and tasting their incredible product has resulted in my rarely making my own tempeh anymore. Sourcing locally from wonderful purveyors who share similar food philosophies is totally the opposite of the corporate model of going to a megamart, buying things that were made in factories far away, shipped, and which then sat on the shelf for absurd amounts of time. By sourcing locally, we help develop our local economy, we meet some wonderful people, support each other's businesses, and maintain some semblance of a sane approach to food and eating. By going to megamarts we make the choice to destroy local economies, as all profit from that megamart and its products gets sucked up the corporate ladder. Every day we are making choices about what we eat and this inevitably impacts others. It is community when I pick up bread from Victor, Rafa, or Jabari, who just pulled it out of the oven at Arizmendi, or if I pick up tofu from Kevin or Minh or tempeh from Melissa. With this particular TAZ, we are demonstrating and producing a model that shows we simply can live without those corporate constraints, and when it comes to food and music, without their horrible products.

The series is inspired by a number of sources, one being the legendary musician Sam Rivers, who, during the 1970s in New York City, held concerts in his loft. I started listening to Sam in my teens, and during my time in graduate school at Florida State University, Sam moved to Orlando. He became a huge source of inspiration for me as a young musician, getting to hear him live numerous times and getting to listen in on his big band rehearsals. Plus, he was constantly asking me about my own work and frequently attended my own performances. Of course, getting the chance to be around such a great, elder master is inspiring to any young musician! But Sam had charisma and influence way beyond the norm and his genuine interest in younger musicians was startling, refreshing, and deeply influential. Talking to him about his loft series was endlessly inspiring, hearing how Sam and his wife, Beatrice, opened up their home to provide young and established musicians a place to perform. In addition, they were providing the audience with a very intimate way to listen to live music: in an intimate setting where the lines of audience and performer are blurred, where communication between listener and performer is quite direct!

Former home of Sam Rivers, Manhattan, NY

Studio Rivbea started offering house concerts in a loft at 24 Bond Street in lower Manhattan in 1970. These musicians, mostly jazz and avant garde performers, and predominantly African American, were taking control of the presentation of music. This was not music designed to sell drinks at a bar, nor to inspire people to get up and dance. The focus was on experimentation, free of any constraints that are often placed by venues, festivals, and the like. A literal who's-who of the jazz/experimental music of the time performed on this series, as well as many younger, unknown musicians, many of whose careers were started or launched at this loft. Studio Rivbea was an essential environment for the cultivation of dozens of brilliant, creative musicians. These musicians found a space where they could perform, rehearse, and commune outside of the typical environments where music is created and presented. A few of them (Oliver Lake, David Murray, Roscoe Mitchell) also performed on my series decades later! Sam and I spoke of him playing on my series but sadly, he never returned to the west coast due to his advanced age. He left us in 2011 at age eighty-eight, after a truly remarkable career as a composer, performer, bandleader, teacher, and mentor.

House-concert series around the United States have become fairly common and popular. In general, they are often limited to the folk and singer-songwriter genres. For some reason, the overwhelming majority of house concerts focus on or are exclusive to this genre. As a musician, I often found myself performing on some of these events when I was collaborating with songwriters, and thought it would be nice to extend this idea to the more experimental forms of music that I was more interested in as a listener and a performer. All I needed to get going was the space.

In 2005, I moved into a loft in West Oakland. With fold-up tables on the walls and a large table for ten in the middle, we were able to fit twenty seats in the space. A simple model was created where I did the cooking, one person helped with plating and prep work, and another assistant did all the serving and cleaning. This model was more recently refined to simply have me and my sous-chef for most of the last six years, Cori Ander, do the roles of what used to be the two of us plus another assistant. Guests immediately noticed and commented on the kitchen, stage, and diners all being in the same space. The open space allowed for open communication. Diners often ask questions or comment to me and my assistants in the kitchen while we are working or plating. Alienation as to how food is prepared was immediately removed from the equation as diners witnessed everything: the steaming, stir-frying, deep-frying, sautéing, mixing, saucing, noodle making, ravioli folding, and every other imaginable kitchen techniques right in front of them. There were two shows, the kitchen and the music! And in some cases, the music and food performances happened simultaneously. Mark Dresser once performed solo while apples were baking in the oven right behind him, the aromas of the spices and wine getting deeper and deeper as the performance went on. And Barre Phillips was quite entertained himself as Cori decorated a cake a couple of feet away from him at the same time as he performed.

A format was established that stuck through all the events: several courses would be served, then, after the entree, we would clear the tables, move the plating table out of the way, and have a concert. Following the concert would be dessert. One reviewer ironically warned people, "If you want dessert, they are going to make you sit through a concert before they serve it to you. And the music is not always easy listening." The real irony of that review was that it was written after a stunningly beautiful Chris Caswell solo harp performance. We never present "easy listening" music on the series, but a concert of harp music from around the world presented by a virtuoso like Chris is not exactly a challenge for most ears.

The first dinner concert took place in August, 2005, and the musical guest was Kurahashi Yoshio (now known as Kurahashi Yodo II), one of the world's greatest shakuhachi players, visiting from Kyoto. Kurahashi-sensei also happens to be my main shakuhachi teacher, thus I wanted him to be the first performer on the series and he has since returned numerous times for repeat performances. The four-course menu and the concert was offered at a ridiculously low price of forty dollars per person, and the twenty seats sold out fairly easily with at least twice as many people wanting to make reservations. The menu consisted of homemade tofu, homemade tempeh, homemade noodles, and more. This became the norm, not only for the underground restaurant but for the catering business in general; most things were handmade! We made practically everything ourselves, from scratch, the day of the dinner. And we took full advantage of the twelve-months-a-year harvest in Northern California. Every menu was based from local ingredients, often sourced directly from farms. There is simply no excuse not to, as it makes no sense not to go all locally sourced when being a chef in a geographical area such as this.

Early in the dinner-concert series history, a woman (Kat) in my cooking class asked a question: "My friend Oliver Lake is going to be in town next month; would you like to have him play solo on your series?" "Put All My Food on the Same Plate" came to mind -- a wonderful poem that Oliver was known to recite in his solo concerts; a poem that I always took to heart as a musician and as a chef! Of course I enthusiastically agreed, having seen Oliver Lake perform a number of times in the World Saxophone Quartet, solo, and with his incredible Trio 3 (with Reggie Workman and Andrew Cyrille). And, not surprisingly, Oliver ended his powerful solo concert with a recitation of that poem. A few years later, his longtime colleague David Murray gave a tremendous solo concert on the series. David grew up in Oakland, so his concert included stories of his experiences growing up and starting to learn music in schools and churches in the neighborhoods. Talk about community! While I sat on the floor about two feet from the bell of David's bass clarinet and tenor saxophone, he charmed the crowd with his powerful playing and his tales of the neighborhoods we were all intimately familiar with. Both Oliver and David mentioned the similarities of what was happening in this loft to what happened at Rivbea studios and other lofts in the '70s in New York City. David said, "But we were lucky to get cheese and crackers, back then. No one was setting up the audiences and musicians with these kinds of plates." As a chef, inspired by music, I have to think of coming up with a wide array of textures and colors and flavors, based upon tradition, yet seeking something new if I want to emulate music masters on such levels as these!

A question that often came up from the guests was, "How do you get these incredible musicians to perform in such a small space?" "I ask them!" is the simple answer. In almost every case, the musicians were friends or colleagues or teachers of mine from my other career as a musician and music teacher. Occasionally, some musicians were asking *me* to play on the series! International music magazine *Signal To Noise* did a feature on the series, as did several local publications, *East Bay Express*, *Oakland Magazine*, and others. Countless people were blogging, positively, about their experiences, yet we managed to stay under the radar for a decade and running! During this decade, sadly, I witnessed almost every other underground restaurant in the Bay Area get a visit from the authorities and thus get shut down. Recently, there are new vegan underground restaurants appearing in the Bay Area! One of them is run by a friend and colleague who often works for my business, and I sometimes work for his, and we have both attended and enjoyed each other's approaches to underground dining. He and his wife are featuring brunches in a beautiful greenhouse setting in Berkeley. Sadly, as I write this, he informs me they are moving and thus will not have this space any longer. Another new one began a year ago, run by a couple new to the Bay Area. These series are all about food, no live music, keeping my series in its own unique space. It is inspiring to see others using a similar model in the area and to experience what they are offering.

One morning, I woke up and checked my email. A message from a musician I absolutely adore but never met nor had any kind of contact with, wrote, "I am going to be in the San Francisco area as a tourist with my husband. I read about your concert series with vegetarian food and would like to perform. I play pipa, a very ancient Chinese instrument." Signed, Yang Jing. WHAT?! I assumed it was a joke being played on me by my friend, Jie Ma, another wonderful pipa player, with whom I had a duet project for many years. Jie had introduced me to Yang Jing's music shortly after we met and started our duet project. After making a phone call I found out Jie was not playing a joke on me and I wrote back readily agreeing, asking for a date and expressing how much I loved her recordings, the solo traditional work, and the brilliant improvised duets with Swiss percussionist Pierre Favre. A few months later, this great Yang Jing had 20 people on the edge of their seats, talking about her personal story with the instrument as a child and her work in Europe and how it led her into new music and improvisation. She kept saying how happy she was to be able to do a concert where she could talk to each person in the audience and discuss her story. Like so many other musicians on the series, Yang Jing represents a tradition that is very much alive and moving forward and in constant transition. As an anthropology student I learned that culture is a process, always in flux. Musicians like Yang Jing make that very obvious, performing music that is hundreds of years old and then improvising pieces that are only for the moment, all in the same concert.

The origin of each menu starts with the musician who is performing that night. I always ask them if they have dietary restrictions and then ask their food loves and dislikes. Some musicians get very interested in this process while others simply leave it to me. One musician got upset with my question and asked, sternly, "I am not asking you what I should perform, so why are you asking me what you should cook?" I understood his sentiment but he was not understanding why I was trying to get his involvement: one, for personal taste, and two, for a collaboration between the kitchen and the performer. Other performers would get very detailed in their interests, and in one case, Arabic violinist Sami Shumays requested an Arabic-Japanese fusion menu.

The most memorable collaboration between the stage and kitchen undoubtedly was the first time Mark Dresser performed on the series. Mark is one of the most incredible bass players of our time and a very kind, warm person. His first appearance on the series was during the eight days of Passover; both of us coming from reform Jewish backgrounds made this time of year laden with memories and meaning. I told him I wanted to run with the theme of traditional Ashkenazi Passover foods. For me, this obviously ties in with childhood memories of stuffed cabbage rolls, matzah ball soups, kugels, tzimmes, charoses, horseradish, and so many delectable treats. And Mark said he would be doing the same, musically. He performed five improvisations/compositions, "Invocation of Elijah" and "The Four Questions" (one piece for each question). He had extensive handwritten notes regarding his experiences as a child with Passover as well as his experiences as a father of a teenager and how the meaning of Passover has evolved for him. Mark's playing is always very personal but being in a very small space, and having him share stories regarding the meaning and intentions of these pieces brought the music to an even higher level. His "Invocation," as more than one member of the audience stated, truly felt like the door had opened and brought in the spirit, and we all did feel a draft come through the crack in the window during this piece. Prior to the concert, the kitchen was bringing out matzah ball soups, collard leaves stuffed with tempeh, and root vegetables with morel and tahini sauces. Cauliflower kugel, charoses made with our friends' Wild Hog Vineyard's Pinot Noir, and a variety of other modernized recipes from my childhood, transformed versions of my Aunt Rose's kitchen, while Mark took his Passover memories and transformed them into beautiful sonic territory.

Mark has since returned to the series for two more solo concerts as well as a duet with vocalist/dancer Jen Shyu. Another highlight of the series occurred when he returned for a duet performance with bass player Barre Phillips, one of my very favorite musicians and someone I had the honor to perform and record with early in my career! This was actually the first time these two giants of the contrabass did a duet concert together!

Another memorable evening was when trombonist Stuart Dempster performed a solo concert. Stuart literally wrote the book on avant-garde trombone techniques and was someone I became familiar with in college through his solo recordings and work with the Deep Listening Band. After moving to the West Coast, I met and performed with Stuart a few times via mutual friends Matthew Sperry and Pauline Oliveros, and discovered he was a very charming, warm man with a childlike playfulness. His motto is to put the play back into playing music and it is quite obvious when you meet him. His solo concert was attended by many of his old friends from his college days in San Francisco at SFSU. In the audience that evening were Terry Riley, Loren Rush, Ramon Sender, and several others of the older generation of West Coast artists whom I grew up admiring. Many of them had been students along with Pauline at Robert Erickson's composition classes, over half a century before this solo performance in my loft. I recall telling my server, Isabelle, that one of our guests is in every music history book and pointed Terry Riley out to her. She said, "You mean the old hippie guy? He and his wife are so sweet!" Yeah, some of our sweet, older guests happened to be absolute geniuses in various art forms that evening! And Stuart charmed us with his wit and stories, and our ears and hearts were treated to the beautiful sounds that can only come out of someone's instrument who has studied for six decades! Stuart recently returned for a second appearance on the series. For this appearance I decided to focus the menu on layers. When I first heard Stuart's solo music, he was playing with a forty-five-second natural reverb. So he would play a note and let it resonate and then layer notes and textures on top of another. So the salad that night had socca crepes layered with fava bean spread, roasted corn and peppers, and olive tapenade. Entree was layered from bottom to top: roasted eggplant slice, smoked eggplant spread, smoked tempeh, homemade almond ricotta, cornmeal-crusted fried eggplant slice, basil pesto, roasted cherry tomato sauce, pine nuts. Dessert had three layers of kanten, the first layer of blueberry juice molded with fresh peaches, the second was cherry juice molded with fresh blueberries, and the top was a coconut-milk mold with fresh blackberries. Trying to emulate the layers of textures in Stuart's music with layers of textures and flavors in the food.

That evening, I asked Terry, who had attended a couple of previous dinner concerts, if he would be interested in performing, and much to my delight he said "Of course." His son, my friend Gyan, who performed on the series a number of times over the years, was in the audience with him that night and the two agreed to do a duet in coming months. Due to the very popular performers, we offered a two-night run of the father-son duet performing raga, as Northern Indian music has long been a study of Terry's, and of course for Gyan as well. When I was sixteen years old my guitar teacher, Pat, introduced me to "A Rainbow In Curved Air," one of Terry Riley's early solo performances. My love of Terry's music constantly evolved over the years, having performed his epic composition, "In C," as a graduate student and also as a professional musician, later in my career. And here was this giant of modern music, with his son, playing for twenty people in my living room, smiling away, and chatting liberally with the audience between pieces. Terry and his wife Ann have since returned to be diners/listeners; always a joy to be in a room with them.

Joëlle Léandre is another musician whom I absolutely adore! When I first began the series she was in residence at Mills College, a few miles away. And we were involved in a few different performance situations, becoming friends, and she was excited to play in my home, where she would sometimes just come by to talk, and of course, to eat. She was the third musician to play on the series in the first year and then returned ten years later on her next visit to California. Her second performance was literally one of the finest of the ten years of concerts in the loft. Music cannot get more real than what Madame Contrabass offers in her solo performances. For decades she has traveled the world, playing solo as well as collaborating with many of the finest composers and improvisors. Watching her set up to play solo is like watching Messi get ready to take a penalty kick. You can see the plan starting to develop as she picks up the bass (in this case, the bass on loan that once belonged to Matthew Sperry), grabs the bow, closes her eyes and begins the journey that only the grandmaster improvisors can take you on. Again, like watching Messi in action, she takes you on journeys one does not think possible to come from a solo contrabass instrumentalist, and afterwards is out of breath from the sheer athleticism involved. Afterwards someone asked, "Did anyone record that?" to which Joëlle said, "No, it is in the ether, sent outwards, where it belongs," followed by her delightful, huge, boisterous laugh and wide smile. Je t'aime, Joëlle, you are a truly special spirit!

One of our regular performers over the years has been electric bass player Michael Manring. Michael is one of the most imaginative musicians one can encounter, literally redesigning the instrument (Zon instruments has the Michael Manring bass commercially available), while being one of the most humble, beautiful people you can encounter. He performs almost every year, always offering something very different, from solo performances of Beethoven Sonatas (yes, one can play "Pathétique" on four strings, though I still can't ponder how he managed to cover all the voices) to some of his own gorgeous compositions.

Numerous shakuhachi players have, of course, been part of the series. My teacher Yodo Kurahashi II (formerly known as Yoshio Kurahashi) was the first performer on the series and has returned six times. Kaoru Kakizakai has played here numerous times, as has the incredible performer Riley Lee. John Neptune, Alcvin Ramos, Cornelius Boots, and Brian Ritchie also appeared on the series, much to the delight of many of the local shakuhachi students, including my own. Between these players, numerous different approaches to traditional and contemporary shakuhachi playing have been performed on this series. More to come, I hope!

A nonmusical collaboration that occurs annually is a multi-course peach menu using heirloom peaches from the Masumoto Family Farm. Interestingly, this collaboration also started through music. Many years ago, I was asked to do a reading of a piece for shakuhachi, koto, narrator, and orchestra with the Oakland Symphony orchestra, composed by William Ludtke. The narrator was a man named David "Mas" Masumoto, who was using texts from his book, *Epitaph for a Peach*. During the rehearsals of the piece, I got to know Mas and immediately was drawn to his gentle, friendly character and his intense enthusiasm for being a farmer, a peach farmer in particular. I learned that he was a third-generation farmer, obviously of Japanese descent. As a lover of peaches, I was curious about his farm, read his book, and could not wait for the season, still a few months away. Later that year, in mid-July I was in Berkeley Bowl, a market locally owned by a Japanese-American family, with perhaps the greatest produce section on the planet, looking at the peach section. There I saw a sign: "Sun Crest Peaches, Masumoto Farm, Del Rey, California." For the first time, I laid eyes on these peaches! Beautiful, large, Rothko-esque colored. Stunningly beautiful were these peaches, unlike anything I had seen. I grabbed a few, barely able to resist sinking my mouth and face right into one. They were expensive, higher priced than the others, but I did not care, I had to try these. After reading the book and talking with Mas, I HAD to try these. As soon as I walked out of the store, I grabbed the ripest one out of my bag. Standing in front of the store, crowds of people walking by, I bit into this peach. And it dripped all over me. My chin was covered, my shirt was getting quite a bit on it, while my mouth had the most exquisite peach flavor imaginable. I think I fell in culinary love with the Masumoto farm during that moment, a love affair that will never end. It deepens every summer when we go through case after case of their harvest and it deepens every time I encounter another member of the delightful Masumoto family.

So every year we present a multi-course menu using the Sun Crest peach from Masumoto farms as the focal point of every course. Raw peaches, smoked peaches, roasted peaches, grilled peaches, all kinds of peach sauces, peach sodas, peaches infused into various alcohols, peaches marinated in various alcohols, peach smoothies, peach teas -- we try to do everything one can do with a peach and it is one of the most fun menus I have ever had a chance to play with. Every year, we contact the farm and ask if Mas can come. Of course he cannot leave the farm in the middle of harvest season but I always want to ask in hopes we can have the farmer join us for the dinner focused on the farm's delightful harvest. In July, 2013, we had the good fortune to have Marcy Masumoto, Mas's wife, attend!

The plan was for Marcy to read from her new cookbook and from other writings by family members between each course. Eight courses of peach dishes were designed! Marcy set the tone, greeting everyone who came in, charming them with her friendly demeanor. We started the menu with the simplest course I ever served: a peach half, unadorned, ungarnished. I introduced the night and then Marcy said a few words about the trees where these Sun Crest peaches came from, planted the year Nikiko, their daughter, was born. She read a couple of paragraphs from Mas's *Epitaph for a Peach*, a book that details the history of the farm and how Mas brought back this amazing heirloom, perhaps the finest of any peach known.

After Marcy read and spoke, she invited everyone to enjoy the Sun Crest Peach in her favorite manner, simply in and of itself. We watched the twenty guests pick up the peach half, bite into it, and then immediately saw everyone smile brightly, followed by picking up napkins and wiping themselves. And then the "wows" and the moans and the sensual sounds that food lovers make when their buttons are pushed and massaged and prodded. The mood was set for a great evening as the tastebuds were scintillated; Marcy was inspiring everyone with stories of the farm, and my sous-chef at the time, Cori, and I were at the peak of our game as a team; peach barbecue sauce with a bottle of Zaya rum in it, served with peach-smoked tempeh, was probably the highlight. Homemade peach sodas poured through the night and no one left for well over an hour after dessert plates were cleared. Food has never been so personalized before for me as it was that evening. Usually I list my sources on the menu of farms, tofu makers, etc. But to have the farmer there, sharing her love of farming, her love of cooking, her love of food, of community -- this night was an overwhelming success and, in some ways, the highlight of my career as a chef. I became a chef because I love food, love sharing food, love eating food, studying food. Over the years, I am very used to getting positive reactions from parties, from classes, and certainly from the underground restaurant diners and listeners. But this night was on a different level. A very different level that will be difficult to surpass.

The Masumotos are a family of artistic, intellectual farmers! After meeting them you get the further understanding of why the food they grow is so good. They truly care about the food, about the people consuming what they grow, about the earth they grow food upon, about their workers who help them run the farm, and it shows in every peach in every box! They do not want to create a peach commodity but want to create peach communities! And one can taste the difference!! There is an old-world charm to this family and their farm. Although Mas is totally

Californian, he is still very Japanese in many regards. During my times in Japan I have encountered many people with a basic goal in life: to do whatever it is they do on the highest possible level. The stereotype of the samurai committing his life to his master is very evident in this philosophy, the master being an art form or a craft or, in this particular case, peach farming. This attitude we do not see enough of in the United States, most obviously. This philosophy and approach is documented very well in the film *Jiro Dreams of Sushi*.

For many of the musicians who have performed on my series, improvisation is an integral aspect of their approach to creating music. Composing without an eraser in real time is an approach to music I have always found intriguing as a listener and as a performer. And this interest extends to the kitchen. Can there be such a thing as free improvisation in the kitchen? Often we start with menus already planned or partly planned. Inevitably this often gets altered once we are at the market and see ingredients that look stunning that we did not expect, or sometimes not seeing what we are hoping for. In the process of cooking itself, improvisation is always a method; altering flavors based on the moment, on the changing weather patterns of the day, on the changing mood or feeling in the kitchen. Recipes are rarely followed to an exact point on purpose, the same way the musicians are not expected to play the same compositions the same way every time. The focus is more on technique and inspiration, using the basics as a point from which to explore; the same way a musician may approach a score is how the kitchen will approach a recipe. And the way musicians sometimes improvise freely on stage, we sometimes start a sauce simply by caramelizing onions, not really sure where we are heading with it till real-time development, the same way a musician approaches a free improvisation.

Many great compositions were based on improvisations in music; the same with some of my recipes. A peach sauce was being made for a Masumoto farm peach event to go with smoked tempeh. This turned into a barbecue sauce with an entire bottle of Zaya rum that was then written down to be remembered since the result was so startling.

Instead of always following recipes, I prefer to develop things spontaneously -- doing what Steve Lacy referred to when he said, "Improvising is like walking on a high wire" -- exploring unknown territory, not knowing if you will easily cross the wire to the other end or fall flat on your face in the process. Improvising is about taking risks, not taking the safe and known route. It is about exploring new territory. What happens when one sound follows another? What happens if you replace makrut lime with yuzu in a Thai curry paste? Once you have made a sound and followed it with another, you have created a relationship. Where to go from there? Once you have combined two flavors, you have created a relationship. Where do you go from there? If you are improvising, you figure out these "problems" at the same time as you reveal your solutions; the audible or culinary results are immediate to the thought process.

With this in mind, please look at the recipes as an improvisor would. Of course, you can make things as written and get wonderful results, but play with it, try to go inside of the "score" (recipe). As a music teacher I stress to my students that the written notes are simply the surface of the piece and we must go inside of the score to find the actual music! The same for a recipe; to truly understand it we must go inside the "score," finding the reasons why the recipe works and then exploring from there. Understand why or how the acid or salt or fat is included and see what can be altered for a different, equal, or better result. Cooking is art and science; in order to go beyond recipes, you have to go into the science of cooking but that goes beyond the scope of this book. Learn and study your basics (scales, long tones, knife work, various cooking techniques), learn basic and traditional compositions (recipes), and then it is time to fly!

Eat and be well.

Philip Gelb, July 2015

Thank you to all the following musicians who have performed on the series. To host such brilliant, talented, and virtuosic performers is a real treat. My apologies for only being able to pay a fraction of what you all deserve to be earning!

Due to the small space, most concerts are solo with occasional duets.
Number indicates the amount of times they have appeared on the series.

Tim Berne - alto saxophone (Brooklyn)
Shay Black - voice, guitar (Berkeley via Ireland)
Cornelius Boots - shakuhachi/bass clarinet
Monique Buzzarte - trombone, electronics (NYC)
Chris Caswell (2) - harp (Berkeley)
Stuart Dempster (2)- trombone (Seattle)
Robert Dick (2) - flute (NYC)
Mark Dresser (2) - bass (Los Angeles)
Mark Dresser/Jen Shyu duet - bass, voice/dance
Mark Dresser/Barre Phillips duet
Sinan Erdemsel - oud (Istanbul)
Sinan Erdemsel/ Sami Shumay duet - oud, violin
Gianni Gebbia - saxophones (Palermo, Italy)
Vinny Golia- winds (Los Angeles)
Lori Goldston - cello (Seattle)
Frank Gratkowski (2) - clarinets, alto sax (Berlin)
Daniel Hoffman/Jeanette Lewicki duet violin, voice/accordion (Berkeley, Tel Aviv)
Shoko Hikage - koto (Japan-San Francisco)
Yang Jing - pipa (Beijing)
Kaoru Kakizakai (4) - shakuhachi (Tokyo)
Marco Lienhard - shakuhachi (Zurich-NYC)
Mari Kimura - violin, electronics (Tokyo-NYC)
Yoshio Kurahashi (Yodo Kurahashi II) (6) - shakuhachi (Kyoto)
Joëlle Léandre (2) - contrebass (Paris)
Oliver Lake - alto sax (NYC)
Riley Lee (2) - shakuhachi (Australia)
Jie Ma - pipa (China, LA)
Thollem Mcdonas/Jon Raskin duet - piano/sax (wanderer/Berkeley)
Roscoe Mitchell - alto, soprano saxophones (Oakland)
David Murray - tenor sax (Paris)
Michael Manring (5) - electric bass (Oakland)
Hafez Modirzadeh - winds (San Jose)
John Kaizan Neptune - shakuhachi (Japan)
Rich O'Donnell - percussion (St. Louis)
Pauline Oliveros (2) - accordion (NY)
Tim Perkis/John Biscoff duet - computers (Berkeley)
Barre Phillips solo and duet with Mark Dresser - contrebass (France)
Alcvin Ramos - shakuhachi (Vancouver)
Tim Rayborn/Annette duet - oud, strings, recorders (Berkeley, Germany)
Jon Raskin/Liz Albee duet - sax/trumpet (Berkeley/Berlin)
Jane Rigler - flute (Colorado)

Gyan Riley (5) - guitar (NYC)
Terry Riley (2) - voice, harmonium (Universe)
Diana Rowan (3) - harp (Berkeley/Ireland)
Bon Singer/Shira Kammen duet - (voice, violin) (Berkeley)
LaDonna Smith/India Cooke duet (2) violin, viola (Birmingham, AL; Oakland)
Lily Storm/Diana Rowan - voice, harp (Oakland/Ireland-Berkeley)
Lily Storm/Dan Cantrell (2) - voice/accordion (Oakland)
Howard Wiley - tenor saxophone solo and duet with Faye Carol voice
Theresa Wong/Ellen Fullman (Berkeley)
Amy X (3) - voice, electronics (Oakland)
Pamela Z - voice, electronics (San Francisco)

ACKNOWLEDGMENTS

Thank you to the recipe testers: Lisa Bromberg, Mark Flanaghan, Todd Jenkins, Sheila Tajima, Tom Deplontey, Elliot Kallen, Kiku Day, Rachel Ridgeway, Sara Baird, Jesse Fujikawa, Lena Strayhorn, Endang Utari, Elliot Budnick, Angela O'Brien, Pax Ahimsa, Ziggy, Lisa Lynne Franco, Shen Robinson.

Thank you to all the musicians who have performed on the series!!! You have all been seriously underpaid to play in this tiny space for 20 eager listeners.

Thank you to friends who have helped me evolve as a cook and chef through the years. Food is always more fun when shared and these are the people I have enjoyed sharing with the most: Cori Ander, Phil Ballman, Scott Walton, Sophie Placard, Kelly Peters, Dana Reason, Miho Kim, Jie Ma, Nobu Sakamoto, and Eri Majima.

To the chefs who have inspired me, particularly Eric Tucker (Millennium restaurant in San Francisco) and my friend, Miyoko Schinner. To the geniuses in the kitchens of my favorite restaurants: Spices 3 Sichuan restaurant in Oakland, Pyung Chang Tofu House in Oakland, Vegetarian Dim Sum House in New York (just to name 3), and, of course, to Aunt Rose who started my love of feeding people at a very young age.

To the regular attendees of the underground restaurant. I can't tell you how much your support has meant to me. These folks have come back over and over through the years: Seth Katz, Beth Fryer, Russell Nelson, Allan Cronin, Frances Winddance, Cynthia Ng, Isabel Schneider, Elliot and Cara Kallen, Mike Villareal and his partner Maite, Chris Jerdonek, Karl and Sue Young, and countless others.

Thank you to Timeless Coffee on Piedmont Avenue in Oakland for the breakfasts, coffees, teas, and letting me take up space writing and editing this book on many mornings.

Thank you to Melissa and Betsy of Rhizocali Tempeh for making some of the finest tempeh on the planet and making it a few blocks from my home!

To the long list of contributors to the crowdsourcing fundraiser to release this book:

Linn Maxwell, Van Nguyen, Beverly Hop, Rob Brown, Candan Soykan, Michael Manring, Lynn Maupin, Steven Bretow, Bridget Jeffrey, Jesse Canterbury, Nancy Burkhardt, Lynn Lampky, Sean Rinehart, Matt Brumit, Angela Coon, Dean Rowan, Stefan Greif, Christina Hoheisel, Nobu Sakamoto, Christoph Maurath, Dave Manson, Sayuri Sakamoto, Peter Fikaris, Clyde Lerner, Inrax Golar, June Watanabe, Bruce Mitchell, Gisela Gamper, Stuart Dempster, Lucia Sheppard, Allison Abresch Meyer, Jeff Alpert, Anna Lum, Rich O'Donnell, Fran Laughton, Myra Chachkin, Alma Chaney, Kiku Day, Peter Kuhn, Mujdat and Nazan Pakan, Kyle and Ashley Knies, Alcia Robb, Cecile Biltekopf, Russ Nelson, Isobel Schneider, Stephanie Morris, Cecily Ward, Eric Tucker, CJ Hafner, Chandresekhar, Ramakrishnan, Amy Coit, Kelly Peters, Kyoko Kitamura, Kristina Gestuvo, Melissa Lane, David Lingren & Ilana Schatz, Howard Wiley, Tat Wong, Tucker Dulin, Santhi Hariprasad, Mark Dresser, Meeranai Shim, Amy Likar, Herb and Ellen Kyler, Mark Werlin and Sarah Paris, Shoko Hikage, Marie Chia and Shane Stanbridge, Dorothy Alpert, Elise and Jeff Delfield, Craig Gottlieb, Seth Katz, Roberta and Phillip Strasbourg, Mike Palatnick, Tam & Karl Ginsberg, Nadine and Karl Schmidt, Lisa Vargas, Arlene Gottlieb, Ilene & Ed Gold, Martha & Marvin Gelb, Debra Flanagan, Scott Walton, Harriet Sperry, Rosanne Pizarro, Pax Gethen, Doug Tygar, Chetana Deorah & Darren Blum, Margot Krouwer, Kelli Granade, Soo Yeon Jang, LaVonne Vashon, Miyoko Schinner, Tim Perkis, Robert & Diana Kehlmann, Eric Ogrey, Allan Cronin, Michael Lindsey, Scott Rosenberg, Donald Bromberg, Saruab, Samdani, Stif Venaas, Stephen Malagodi, Ursula Fritsch, Tom Deplontey, Mara Ann Hagerty, Emily Huston, Alicia Smiley, Ed Pizzi, Takeshi Oda, Garland Withers, JoAnne Goldberg, Sheila Tajima Shadle, Amy Neuburg, Nomi Dekel, Dav Yaginuma, Michael Kobb, Laura Verduzco, Ken Shultz, Ellen Fullman, Jesse Miner, Julie Thompson, Erin Pinto, Jason Ditzian, James Black, Arlene Kyler and Daniel Schoenfeld of Wild Hog Vineyards.

Special thank you to Eve Lynch for editorial work on this book, Dyanna Csaposs for the layout and design work, cover photo by Rebecca Martinez, and Chetana Deorah for photos as well as website design.

To my long-time sous-chef, Cori Ander, for putting up with me, for the amazing cakes, and of course, the inspiration of cooking together!

To my neighbors who have put up with music and aromas wafting into their lofts and not complaining or calling the authorities. And to the one exception, the neighbor's guest who lost it in the middle of a LaDonna Smith solo, pounding on the walls and then a window, only to inspire LaDonna to get louder and more frantic on her viola.

To my various clients over the years who have trusted me to cook food for their special events.

This book is dedicated to the memory of Matthew Sperry. Although it is over a dozen years since he left, thoughts of him are constantly with me. We were roommates in music school and great friends from then on, performing together as a duet and in various ensembles together in many parts of the country. I inspired Matt to love to cook, which he shared with his wife Stacia and his countless friends. When he passed I was just starting to make the transition from hobbyist home cook to professional chef. I often come up with new ideas, thinking, "What would Matt think of this one?" Matt's presence is often felt in my kitchen, his warm smile looking down, nodding in approval. His bass has been used in concerts by three great masters who performed on the series, Joëlle Léandre, Mark Dresser, and Barre Phillips.

GLOSSARY

These days, everything is available online! So if you are not in a major city with large immigrant populations, you can still have access to the entire world of food. If you are in a major city, befriend your local "ethnic" markets. You will usually be met with great kindness and big smiles if you walk into places and start asking for and purchasing traditional ingredients.

Asafoetida: Also known as "hing." Made from the resin of a tree, this is used in small amounts for intense flavor. It is a substitute for garlic and onions in some Hindu vegetarian cuisines. Easy to find in Indian grocery stores or online.

Ashkenazi: Branch of Jews from Eastern Europe.

Chinkiang vinegar: A black vinegar from China, made from rice and aged in barrels. Very strong and intense tasting, thus is used sparingly. An integral flavor to many Chinese dishes and sauces.

Choy sum: A delicious leafy green, found in many Asian cuisines.

Epazote: Mexican herb. Found fresh in season, but dried is also good.

Fermented bean curd: A cheesy type of aged tofu, intensely flavored, thus used sparingly. The red fermented bean curd is aged with dates and is an integral part of char siu sauce.

Fermented black beans: Salted and dried black beans from China, easily found in Asian markets.

Gai lan: Also known as Chinese broccoli.

Green papaya: An unripe papaya used to make salads in Vietnam, Thailand, and other Southeast Asian culinary traditions.

Kabocha: Japanese word for pumpkin and also the name of the flavorful green pumpkin used in many of my recipes.

Kanten (agar agar): A seaweed-derived extract that comes in bars, powder, or flakes. Used for thickening and for a variety of Japanese sweets.

Koji: Another wonderful ingredient from the traditional Japanese kitchen. A type of mold that is grown on rice or other grains or beans to use as a fermenting agent. Used to make miso, sake, mirin, shoyu, tamari, and many other integral ingredients in the Japanese kitchen. Koji can also be used as a pickling base for vegetables.

Kombu: A seaweed found in the Pacific that is used for a variety of culinary purposes, stocks being one of the main ones. Kombu stock is simple to make and very flavorful.

Kudzu: A Japanese starch from a root. Very healthy and gives a wonderful texture. Yes, the same kudzu that has taken over the South has a wide array of culinary, fiber, energy, and other uses.

Makrut limes: An amazing lime from Thailand, formerly known as kaffir lime. The leaves are used all year round while the juice is used during season, when available. Leaves can be dried or frozen for long storage.

Matcha: Japanese green tea powder used for the tea ceremony. Has a very intense color and bittersweet flavor.

Mirin: A sweet sake from Japan. Difficult to find but worth looking for is Hon Mirin, which is naturally fermented. Most of what is on the market is simply sugar and alcohol, not very tasty or healthy.

Miso: One of Japan's great exports to the world. Naturally fermented miso is one of the world's healthiest foods and is consumed daily by many Japanese. There are dozens of varieties of miso, from very light and sweet to very dark and salty. The darker the miso, the more aged it is.

Nigari: A salt derived from a seaweed, and used in tofu making. This salt helps separate the curds from the whey.

Oil for deep-frying: Deep-frying requires temperatures of 350-385°F, thus we must only use oils that can withstand these temperatures and not impart any flavor. Many oils are excellent for deep-frying, such as: rice bran, coconut, peanut, grapeseed, cottonseed, canola, soybean, and corn.

Ong choy: Also known as water spinach.

Palm sugar: A traditional sweetener in Southeast Asia made from coconut trees.

Red fermented bean curd: A fermented tofu aged with dates and brine. Essential for char siu sauce and other Chinese dishes.

Rejuvelac: A fermented water made from soaking grains, such as rye or amaranth. Used to make nut cheeses, yogurts, and more.

Satsuma imo: A white sweet potato native to the Satsuma region of Kyushu Island, Japan. In winter one can still find pushcarts with men roasting these delicious root vegetables over coals.

Shaoshing: A type of aged rice wine from China.

Shochu: A distilled beverage made from rice, barley, or sweet potato.

Sichuan peppercorns: An incredible spice from Sichuan province, China, that gives a citrusy and numbing spicy effect.

Tamarind extract: If you have access to fresh tamarind (I rarely do), please make your own extract. Most of us are stuck with what we find in stores and we can find tamarind liquid, tamarind extract, tamarind concentrate, tamarind paste, and sometimes frozen tamarind. My recipes all call for a tamarind concentrate that I have seen all over the US and Canada.

Tempeh: A naturally fermented soybean cake that has been a traditional food in Indonesia for 1500 years. In the United States many small tempeh makers are making tempeh from black beans, chickpeas, and other beans and sometimes adding grains as well. Seek out a local tempeh maker whenever possible, as the difference between packaged tempeh on the shelves and the freshly made unpasteurized version is immense. If you are in the San Francisco Bay area, please seek out my friends at Rhizocali Tempeh for some truly outstanding tempeh.

Tien tsen chilis: Skyward-facing peppers, native to Sichuan province, China. These very flavorful and very hot peppers are easily found dried, but rarely found fresh.

Tofu: Found all over Asia and used widely in all Asian cuisines. Tofu comes in a wide array of textures, from silken to very firm. The differences are the water content, with silken not being pressed at all, and the firmer ones having more water pressed out. Tofu is a 4000-plus-year-old tradition!

Yama imo: A Japanese root vegetable used in a wide variety of traditional ways. When grated, it resembles egg whites and thus can be used as a binder. Also wonderful pickled or grated in soba.

Yuba: Japanese word for "tofu skin," the delicate thin layer that rises to the top of the surface when simmering soy milk to make tofu.

Yuzu: A Japanese lime that is not comparable to any other citrus. An early season variety, its skin is as desirable as its juice.

BASICS, STAPLES & SAUCES

SOY MILK

Making your own soy milk produces a fresher, tastier product. It is less expensive to make your own and ecologically logical too, since fewer boxes and containers are produced, thrown away, or recycled. Whenever we make our own staples we reduce our ecological footprint!

YIELD: ABOUT 1 1/2 QUARTS

1 cup dried soybeans

Soak soybeans in water to cover for 8 hours or overnight. Rinse and drain. Bring the soaked soybeans and 4 cups water to a boil and boil them for 10 minutes. Rinse and drain again.

Pour the parboiled soybeans and 4 cups fresh water into a blender and blend on high till thoroughly pureed. Strain the liquid through cheesecloth to remove all solids, and reserve the "milk." Pour the strained solids back into the blender and add 3 more cups of water. Blend till smooth and once again, pass this through cheesecloth. Combine the two milks.

CASHEW CREAM

One of the basics of the vegan kitchen. Cashew cream can be used in so many soups and sauces!

YIELD: ABOUT 3 CUPS

2 cups raw cashews

Soak cashews overnight with at least 3 times the amount of water as cashews. Drain and rinse. Add cashews to a high speed blender with 2 cups of fresh water and process till very smooth. Best if used fresh but can be refrigerated, covered tightly, for up to 3 days.

COCONUT MILK

The flavor of freshly made is always far superior to what we find in a can.

YIELD: ABOUT 5 CUPS

1 coconut
8 cups boiling water

Preheat oven to 350°F. With a chisel and hammer, knock out the 3 eyes of the coconut. Pour out the water into a bowl and save or drink immediately for a very refreshing taste.

Place coconut in oven and bake 10-15 minutes. We do not want to cook the coconut, just heat it so the flesh separates from the shell. Smash the coconut in half, then with a butter knife carefully remove the coconut flesh from its shell.

Place the coconut flesh in a high-speed blender and add 4 cups boiling water. Process on high for 2 minutes. Let rest 10 minutes. Pour the coconut milk into a strainer lined with cheesecloth, placed over a large bowl. Press all the "milk" out of the coconut and add the coconut meat back to the blender. Add 4 more cups boiling water and process on high for 2 minutes, then let it rest for 10 minutes and pour through cheesecloth. Combine the two milks.

HOW TO ROAST AND PUREE A PUMPKIN

This is one of the most important fundamental recipes. Pureed pumpkin is so versatile and is used constantly in my kitchen during the fall and winter seasons. This takes a small amount of effort but the results more than make up for it, especially in comparison to what one finds in a can on supermarket shelves.

Use a sugar pie pumpkin, the small orange pumpkin.

Cut the pumpkin in half. Scoop out the seeds and membrane and save the seeds for roasting. Lightly salt the pumpkin, massaging the salt into the flesh. Place pumpkin in a roasting pan, add 1/2 cup water to the pan, and cover very tightly. Roast at 425°F for 45 minutes. Scoop the pumpkin flesh away from the skin, discarding the skins, and puree in a food processor or mash with a potato masher or fork.

Pies, sorbets, breads, soups, and so much more are now ready to be created with your pumpkin puree.

HOW TO SKIN A PEACH, EASILY

For many recipes, the fuzzy peel of a peach is not desirable. The easiest way to remove the skin is very simple. Make an x, about 1/4 inch deep, on one end of a peach. Drop the peach in rapidly boiling water for 10 seconds. Remove peach and run under cold water to stop the cooking process. The skin will easily peel from where the x was made.

HOW TO MAKE YUZU BOWLS

Yuzu, the Japanese lime, is becoming easier to find in the United States. More farmers are starting to grow this incredible fruit, famous for its distinct aroma and flavor!

These bowls are not edible but they are beautiful and add aroma and some flavor.

Cut off the top of a yuzu, about 1/2 inch from the top. Delicately, scoop out the flesh and seeds and pulp of the yuzu, saving this for sorbet or various other yuzu recipes. Save the tops!

After plating, spooning a stew or curry into the yuzu, you can then add the lid and present it at the table as a whole piece of fruit. The guests can then open the top to see what lies within!

HOW TO MAKE DUMPLING SQUASH BOWLS

Dumpling squashes are incredibly sweet. When you roast them, the sugars and colors really come out yet they are sturdy enough to use as bowls for soups and stews. They pair beautifully with spicy bean dishes and spicy curries as the sweetness of pumpkin always pairs well with spicy chili peppers!

Cut off the top of the squash. Scoop out the seeds and membrane. Save the seeds for roasting! Save the lid! Lightly salt each squash. Place in a roasting pan, add 1/2 cup of water to the pan, cover tightly and roast at 425°F for 30 minutes.

After plating and filling, put the lid back on the pumpkin and take the dish to the table with the lid on. Guests can then open the pumpkin to see what treats await them.

Note: This method also works for delicata squash, carnival pumpkin, and other pumpkins similar in size to dumpling squash.

SWEET AND SOUR SAUCE

Great for accompanying fried wontons or other types of Asian dumplings.

YIELD: ABOUT 1 1/2 CUPS

1 tablespoon coconut oil
1 red onion, diced small
2-20 Thai chilis, minced (for a very hot sauce add the larger number of chilis)
2 teaspoons ginger, minced finely
5 large ripe plums (or peaches, nectarines, apricots, or a combination), diced small
1/4 cup rice vinegar
3 tablespoons palm sugar
1/2 teaspoon sea salt
1 clove
1/8 teaspoon star anise

In a saucepan, heat up coconut oil. Add onion and cook for 10 minutes over medium-low heat, covered, stirring occasionally. Add chili, ginger, and plums, cover, and cook 15 minutes or till fruit is totally broken down. Add the rest of the ingredients, bring to a simmer, cover, lower heat, and cook 1/2 hour. Remove clove.

The results will vary greatly, depending on the quality of fruit you have. Always taste your results and adjust. I am used to using ultra ripe stone fruits in California, so I do not need to add much sweetener to sauces like this to get a desirable flavor. Play around and experiment. Some prefer this sauce more tart, others sweeter, and others through-the-roof hot. I prefer tartness on top followed by heat, with sweetness holding it all together underneath.

SWEET VINEGAR SAUCE

A very simple Thai sauce. This sauce is amazing with freshly fried tofu or tempeh!

YIELD: ABOUT 1 CUP

1/2 cup rice vinegar
1/2 cup palm sugar
1/4 teaspoon sea salt

In a saucepan combine the 3 ingredients and whisk till dissolved. Over low heat, stirring occasionally, bring the sauce to a simmer. Reduce the sauce in volume by half, till it becomes a slightly thick syrup.

Options: Add cucumber and toasted peanuts and cilantro.

PEANUT SAUCE

One of Thailand's great sauces!

YIELD: ABOUT 3 CUPS

1 stalk lemongrass
2 cloves garlic
2 green onions
1 teaspoon fresh minced ginger
2 red Thai chilis
1/4 cup palm sugar
1/4 cup soy sauce
3 tablespoons tamarind liquid
1 cup toasted peanuts
2 cups coconut milk
2 sheets nori
1 tablespoon Chinese fermented bean curd
Vegetable stock if needed

Peel off and discard the outside layer of lemongrass and then cut the interior stalk into 1/2-inch pieces. Combine all ingredients in a blender and blend till smooth. Add this mixture to a saucepan and bring to simmer over medium-low heat, stirring often to prevent sticking. After it starts to bubble, lower heat and, stirring constantly, cook for 10 minutes, adding stock if it becomes too thick.

TAMARIND SAUCE

Goes great with spring rolls in particular! Or just as a dip for fried tempeh.

YIELD: ABOUT 1 1/2 CUPS

2 tablespoons coconut oil
1 onion, minced
2 teaspoons ginger, minced
3 cloves garlic, minced
2 Thai chilis, minced
1/4 cup tamarind extract
20 basil leaves
1/3 cup palm sugar
1/4 cup soy sauce
1 teaspoon coriander powder
1/2 cup Southeast Asian stock (page 98)

In a hot wok, add coconut oil. Add onion, ginger, garlic, and chili and stir-fry 3 minutes. Add the rest of the ingredients and stir-fry 1 minute. Puree this sauce in a blender till very smooth.

SICHUAN CHILI OIL

A hot oil that can add instant flavor to many dishes.

YIELD: ABOUT 2 1/2 CUPS

1 tablespoon Sichuan peppercorns
1/2 cup dried tien tsen chilis
2 cups untoasted sesame oil
1 star anise
1 bay leaf

Heat up a wok. Add peppercorns and chili. Make sure you have a well ventilated space or you will soon be gasping from the pepper gas. Stir-fry till they are very aromatic and fragrant, about 2 minutes. Remove from heat and mash down in a mortar and pestle or food processor. Add the ground peppercorns and chilis to the oil and add this mixture back to the wok. Heat up till it simmers, then lower heat and cook 2 minutes. Place in a glass container, and add a small piece of star anise and a bay leaf. Keep in a cool, dark space for 2 weeks before using.

Variations: Add black cardamom, white peppercorns, cinnamon stick, or clove.

ROMESCO SAUCE

From Spain, this amazing summer sauce is a big favorite for my catering clients and cooking class students. Another fairly easy sauce to make with exceptional results.

YIELD: ABOUT 3 CUPS

1/3 cup raw almonds
4 large ripe red bell peppers
1 ripe tomato
2 tablespoons red wine vinegar
1 teaspoon sea salt
Black pepper to taste
1 teaspoon smoked paprika
1 teaspoon ancho chili powder
1/4 cup extra-virgin olive oil

Blanch almonds for 30 seconds in a pot of boiling water. Rinse in cold water. Remove skins by gently squeezing the almonds, one at a time. Discard skins and place almonds in a blender.

On a barbecue, grill your peppers till completely scorched all around (or roast, covered, at 425°F for 1 hour, turning one-quarter of the way around every 15 minutes so all sides get scorched). Remove skins, cut in half, and remove seeds. Discard seeds and skins. Add roasted peppers to the blender. Add all ingredients except olive oil to the blender and puree till very smooth. Open top, and while blender is running, slowly pour olive oil in. Taste!

Variation: Use different kinds of peppers for quite a variety of flavors.

BASIC TOMATO SAUCE

Summertime heaven!

YIELD: ABOUT 1 1/2 QUARTS

2 tablespoons olive oil
1 onion, chopped
2 teaspoons sea salt
20 ripe tomatoes, chopped
1 carrot, chopped
1 stalk celery, chopped
10 cloves garlic, minced
1 teaspoon dried oregano
1 teaspoon dried thyme
1 teaspoon dried rosemary
1/2 bottle dry red wine
1 teaspoon crushed black pepper
1 bunch basil, leaves removed from stems

In a saucepan, heat up olive oil, add onions and salt, and sauté 10 minutes over medium-low heat. Add tomatoes, carrot, celery, garlic, oregano, thyme, and rosemary. Cook another 10 minutes, stirring often. Add wine and stir well. Over low heat, let this simmer for as long as you can (minimum one hour but longer simmering makes a richer flavored sauce), stirring often. Puree the sauce in a blender, adding black pepper and basil. Season to taste.

Variation: Pomegranate Tomato Sauce

To the above recipe, add 1/4 cup pomegranate molasses and omit the red wine.

PEACH SALSA

I love peaches. My favorite fruit and my favorite peaches come from my friends at Masumoto Farms in Del Rey, California, a 4th-generation Japanese-American Farm. Every summer, I come up with new peach dishes to create a multi-course peach menu using the beautiful heirlooms from their farm, particularly the Sun Crest heirloom, perhaps the juiciest, tastiest peach ever cultivated.

This is a simple, easy-to-make salsa and goes well with a variety of dishes, including of course tacos, tamales, enchiladas, or anything Mexican or Southwestern.

YIELD: ABOUT 3 CUPS

3 Sun Crest or other midsummer heirloom peach, ripe!
3 tomatoes; use a variety of heirlooms, if possible!
1 green onion, chopped
1/4 red onion, chopped
1-3 serrano chilis, chopped
3 tablespoons lime juice
1/2 teaspoon sea salt
2 tablespoons cilantro, chopped

Peel the peaches (see page 30). Remove pit, dice in small pieces. Combine the peaches with the rest of the ingredients and mix gently. Chill for an hour before serving.

GREEN SALSA

Another classic from our neighbors to the south. Mexico once had a thriving, mostly vegetarian, diet, prior to conquest. Spanish imperialism brought cattle ranching and pig farming to many areas and completely changed the local cuisines of Mexico, Argentina, Philippines, Cuba, and elsewhere. The conquest by Spain of the area now known as Mexico had an enormous impact on global cuisine. A huge list of ingredients was first exported from the vast variety of indigenous plants to the rest of the planet, shortly after conquest. This list includes, but is certainly not limited to, tomatoes, corn, chili, chocolate, vanilla, pumpkins, and most beans. Imagine Italian food with no tomatoes or polenta? Thai or Sichuan food with no chili? The whole world with no chocolate or vanilla?

Mexico is home to a variety of different indigenous cultures and thus a variety of culinary traditions. This is one of many ways to make a green salsa, very easy to produce. You have to love sauces that are all about throwing things in a food processor and hitting the button.

YIELD: ABOUT 3 CUPS

10 tomatillos, husked and quartered

1 small onion, quartered

1 clove garlic, minced

1 jalapeño, split, NOT seeded, and quartered (more if you like hot!)

3 tablespoons cilantro

1 teaspoon sea salt

3 tablespoons lime juice

Add all ingredients to a food processor. Pulse till mostly chopped; leave very slightly chunky. Taste! Add salt or more lime if needed. Alternatively, add all ingredients to a mortar and pestle and process it down.

HOW TO MAKE AMAZAKE

Amazake is often used as a drink. It is also the basis for making sake and mirin. Koji is an amazing microorganism used in a variety of traditional Japanese ingredients. It is used to make most types of miso, tamari, shoyu, some pickles, and numerous other integral ingredients in traditional Japanese cuisine. Koji is rice (or sometimes made with other grains or soybeans) that has been inoculated with a type of aspergillus mold. Unlike most types of aspergillus, koji is very healthy to consume and has been a part of traditional Japanese cuisine for many centuries!

YIELD: ABOUT 8 CUPS

2 cups brown mochi kome (a Japanese variety of sweet rice)
3 cups koji

Cook the 2 cups mochi kome with 6 cups water over low heat, covered, for 1 hour. Let cool completely. Cooling the rice is necessary or the high heat will kill the koji! Add koji and mix thoroughly.

Incubate at 140°F using a dehydrator: Wrap the amazake up tightly and place in dehydrator at 140°F for 18 hours or till very sweet. The koji breaks down the rice into a very sweet mixture.

HOW TO MAKE MIRIN (SWEET COOKING SAKE)

YIELD: ABOUT 1 GALLON

1 batch of Amazake (page 41)
1 gallon shochu

In a large fermenting vessel, combine amazake and
shochu. Cover tightly and place in a cool, dark place
for 2-4 months. Uncover, filter the solid particles out
through cheesecloth, and discard solids. Bottle the liquid.
Will keep for 2 years in a cool, dark place.

CASHEW CHÈVRE

Credit where credit is due. I learned this from an amazing chef and cookbook author, my friend Miyoko Schinner. Please check out her books for a lot of great ideas and recipes.

This is an incredibly easy to make nut cheese. The results are quite like a goat milk chèvre, surprisingly. I have even served this to French people who were thrilled, excited, and confused at the results.

YIELD: ABOUT 3 CUPS

3 cups raw cashews
1/2 teaspoon sea salt
1/2 cup rejuvelac

Soak cashews for 6 hours in water to cover. Drain and rinse.

In a high speed blender, process cashews, salt, and rejuvelac till very smooth. You will probably have to stop your machine and scrape down the sides a few times.

Place this mixture in a nonmetallic bowl, cover with cheesecloth, and let sit at room temperature for 3 days to ferment. Refrigerate for a couple of hours before serving.

CHÈVRE ROLLED IN HERBS

YIELD: ABOUT 30 BALLS

1/2 cup chopped chives
1/2 cup chopped chervil
1 tablespoon green peppercorns, crushed
1 recipe Cashew Chèvre (page 43)

Combine the chervil and chives and peppercorns
in a bowl. Using a small ice cream scoop, make tiny
balls of chèvre. Roll in the herb/peppercorn mixture.
Refrigerate before serving to keep the balls firm.

PESTO

YIELD: ABOUT 2 CUPS

4 cups basil leaves
1 cup high quality olive oil
1/2 cup walnuts or pine nuts
3 cloves garlic
2 teaspoons salt
1/2 teaspoon black pepper

In a mortar and pestle or food processor, pulverize all
ingredients into a paste.

ALMOND RICOTTA

This is the first nut cheese I learned to make and still a very common one in my kitchen.

YIELD: ABOUT 3 CUPS

1/2 cup raw almonds
1 cup boiling water
1 tablespoon lemon juice
2 teaspoon maple syrup
1 tablespoon olive oil
1/2 teaspoon sea salt
5 tablespoon kudzu or 1/4 cup cornstarch

Bring a pot of water to a boil and drop raw almonds into the pot and boil for 30 seconds, then immediately drain and rinse almonds with cold water. Remove almond skins by gently squeezing the nuts between your fingers. Discard skins.

Place almonds in a high speed blender with 1 cup boiling water and process for 5 minutes. You must blend the nuts completely into a liquid, thus the long processing time. Add lemon juice, maple syrup, olive oil, and salt and blend well.

In a separate bowl, combine kudzu and 1 cup water and set aside. In a saucepan, add the nut mixture and the kudzu mixture and whisk together. Cook at low heat till the mixture starts to simmer and thicken. Once it begins bubbling, stir continuously for 2 minutes. This last step is needed or you will get a starchy flavor, which is not desirable.

Place mixture in a glass bowl, cover, and refrigerate at least 2 hours.

CRANBERRY YUZU SAUCE

My yuzu-infused take on an American classic. Cranberry season is brief and so worth looking forward to. Cranberry is one of the great flavors associated with the Thanksgiving holiday in the United States and American late fall/early winter menus.

YIELD: ABOUT 3 CUPS

3 cups fresh cranberries
1 yuzu, cut in half, seeds removed (only use organic citrus or you are adding a serious amount
   of pesticides to your sauce and the taste is very obvious)
1/2 cup maple syrup
Dash salt
1 vanilla bean, split

In a saucepan add all ingredients. Bring to simmer over low heat.
Cover, stirring frequently, and cook 30 minutes or till cranberries have
collapsed. Taste. Add more maple if needed.

Options: If yuzu is not available, use half an orange and half a lime.

PEACH MUSTARD

YIELD: ABOUT 1/2 CUP

1/4 cup yellow mustard powder
2 tablespoons soy sauce
1 tablespoon mirin
1 ripe peach, peeled and pitted

In a blender, puree all ingredients with 2 tablespoons water.
Place in a bowl, cover, and let sit half an hour before serving.

STOUT MUSTARD

YIELD: ABOUT 4 CUPS

I love mustard and I love a good stout on a cold winter night.

1/2 cup yellow mustard seeds
1/2 cup brown mustard seeds
1 1/2 cups malt vinegar
1 bottle stout beer (use a low hop, high malt stout)
1/3 cup agave or maple syrup
2 teaspoons allspice
1 cup yellow mustard powder
2 teaspoons sea salt
1 teaspoon turmeric

Combine mustard seeds, malt vinegar, and stout in a bowl; cover and let sit one day. Combine this mixture with the remaining ingredients and 1 1/2 cups water in a blender and puree. Pour back into a bowl, cover, and let age 1 week before serving.

PEACH RUM BARBECUE SAUCE

This was first developed as a total improvisation for one of the annual Masumoto Peach dinners.

YIELD: ABOUT 1 QUART

4 peaches, very ripe
2 tablespoons olive oil
1 onion, minced
2 teaspoons sea salt
4 tomatoes, chopped
5 cloves garlic, minced
1 jalapeño, minced
1 carrot, chopped
1 stalk celery, chopped
1/2 cup maple syrup
1 teaspoon sweet paprika
1 teaspoon smoked paprika
1 teaspoon coriander
1/8 teaspoon clove
1/4 teaspoon cinnamon
1/2 teaspoon allspice
1 1/2 cups dark rum
Vegetable stock as needed

Peel peaches (see page 30). Chop them and set aside.

In a saucepan, heat up olive oil. Add onions and sea salt, cover, and cook over low heat for 20 minutes, till onions are caramelized. Add tomatoes, garlic, peaches, jalapeño, carrots, and celery. Cover and cook 5 minutes. Add the rest of the ingredients, cover, and simmer over low heat for several hours. Stir often to prevent sticking, adding vegetable stock if it gets too thick. Puree sauce before serving or using in a recipe.

WALNUT SAGE SAUCE

Ideal for pumpkin gnocchi (page 88) or fettuccine.

YIELD: ABOUT 3 CUPS

1 cups walnuts
1 clove garlic
1 teaspoon sea salt
2 cups rice or soy milk
Several fresh sage leaves and branches
1/2 teaspoon freshly grated nutmeg

In a cast iron skillet, over medium-low heat, toast the walnuts, stirring constantly until they smell aromatic. Remove from heat and place in a blender with the garlic, salt, and rice milk. Put the pureed ingredients in a saucepan on the stove and add sage leaves.

Over low heat, stirring regularly, bring to a simmer. Keep simmering and stirring till the sauce thickens slightly. Add nutmeg and serve.

Variation: Replace sage with rosemary or marjoram.

ROASTED GARLIC TAHINI SAUCE

YIELD: ABOUT 1 1/4 CUPS

20 cloves garlic, peeled
2 tablespoons grapeseed oil
1 teaspoon sea salt
1/2 cup tahini
1/3 cup olive oil
1/4 cup lemon juice
1/2 teaspoon ground cumin
1/4 teaspoon ground coriander
1/2 teaspoon freshly ground black pepper

In a roasting pan, add garlic, grapeseed oil, and salt. Wrap tightly. Roast at 425°F for 45 minutes, being careful not to burn. Add roasted garlic and the rest of ingredients in a food processor and puree till smooth. Season with more salt and lemon if needed.

MOLE SAUCE

There are infinite varieties of mole sauces. Regional variations all over Mexico are found as well as dramatic variations from chef to chef and from grandmother to grandmother.

YIELD: ABOUT 3 CUPS

2 tablespoons almonds, toasted
2 tablespoons pine nuts, toasted
2 tablespoons pecans, toasted
4 dried ancho chilis, soaked overnight
2-8 dried arbol chilis, soaked overnight (the more you add, the hotter the sauce)
1/4 cup dried apricots, soaked overnight
1/4 cup raisins, soaked overnight
3 tablespoons olive oil
1 onion, chopped
1 teaspoon sea salt
4 cloves garlic, minced
1 carrot, chopped
5 tomatoes, chopped
1 red bell pepper, chopped
2-4 jalapeños, chopped (the more you add, the hotter the sauce)
1 cinnamon stick
1 clove
2 allspice berries
1 teaspoon cumin powder
2 teaspoons oregano
1 teaspoon marjoram
2 tablespoons cocoa powder

Toast the nuts in a pan, over low heat, shaking continuously for 2 minutes or till a nutty aroma is wafting towards your nose.

Remove stems and seeds from the soaked chilis. Drain and save the soaking water from the chilis and dried fruit!

In a hot saucepan, add olive oil. Add onions and sea salt and sauté 5 minutes. Add garlic, carrots, tomatoes, bell pepper, and jalapeños, and sauté another 5 minutes. Add spices (cinnamon, clove, allspice, cumin, oregano, marjoram) and mix well. Add the soaking liquids from the dried fruit and chilis.

In a blender, add the soaked fruit, soaked chilis, cocoa powder, and toasted nuts. Puree this mixture, adding the sauce from the pot till very smooth. Place the pureed sauce back into the saucepan.

Now the secret to a great mole is to simmer this over a very low heat for hours, stirring at least every minute to prevent sticking. It is worth the effort!!

APPLESAUCE

A must for accompanying latkes! I used to hate applesauce. As a kid, my mom used to crush my chemotherapy (childhood leukemia) medicine into applesauce, before I was able to swallow pills. Took years to get over this food trauma! Now I can't imagine not making applesauce when I make latkes!

YIELD: ABOUT 3 CUPS

4 apples (I like to use Empire, Piñata, Cameo, Gala, Fuji, or a combination!)
1 cinnamon stick
1/2 lemon, seeds removed
1 vanilla bean, split
1/4 cup maple syrup
Dash sea salt

Peel, core, dice, and chop apples. In a small saucepan add all ingredients. Over low heat, covered, cook till the apples are completely collapsed, about 40 minutes. Remove lemon, cinnamon stick, and vanilla bean. You can leave the applesauce chunky or puree till smooth.

CHINESE-STYLE MUSTARD

I LOVE mustard and make a variety of Asian- and European-style mustards for many events. There are a wide variety of mustard powders and seeds available on the market so experiment with what you have available locally (and online!) to find your favorites.

YIELD: ABOUT 1/3 CUP

1/4 cup yellow mustard powder

Whisk mustard powder with 1/4 cup water. Cover, and let sit half an hour before serving.

Option: Replace 2 tablespoons water with 2 tablespoons soy sauce.

CHERRY MUSTARD

YIELD: ABOUT 1/2 CUP

1/4 cup yellow mustard powder
2 tablespoons soy sauce
1 tablespoon mirin
1/4 cup pitted, fresh cherries

In a blender, puree all ingredients with 2 tablespoons water. Place in a bowl, cover, and let sit half an hour before serving.

BLUEBERRY MUSTARD

YIELD: ABOUT 1/2 CUP

1/4 cup yellow mustard powder
2 tablespoon soy sauce
1 tablespoon mirin
1/4 cup fresh blueberries

In a blender, puree all ingredients with 2 tablespoons water. Place in a bowl, cover, and let sit half an hour before serving.

SCHUG (YEMENITE HOT SAUCE)

Trying to imitate the amazing hot sauce at the legendary Mamoun's Falafel in NYC.

YIELD: ABOUT 2 CUPS

20 serrano chilis
1 clove garlic
2 tablespoons cilantro
1 teaspoon caraway seeds
1/8 teaspoon cardamom
1/2 teaspoon sea salt
2 tablespoons olive oil
1 tablespoon lemon juice or vinegar

In a mortar and pestle, grind down the chili peppers, garlic, cilantro, and caraway into a paste. Add the rest of the ingredients and mix well.

APPETIZERS

GREEN PAPAYA SALAD

I learned this dish while a graduate student, after watching the beautiful film *"Scent of the Green Papaya."* During many scenes in this film, this dish is created.

Green papaya is an unripe papaya. One can find these at many Asian markets or Thai/Vietnamese markets in particular. To prepare the papaya: peel it first, then cut in half and scoop out the seeds. Shred the papaya with a grater or food processor.

This is entirely raw except for the toasted peanuts. Raw peanuts are not as tasty nor do they offer the same wonderful texture.

YIELD: SERVES 4

Salad:
1 medium green papaya, peeled, seeded, shredded
1 carrot, shredded
4 Chinese long beans, cut into 1-inch pieces
2 cloves garlic, minced

Dressing:
1-6 red Thai chilis, minced
1 teaspoon ginger juice
1/4 cup palm sugar
1/4 cup soy sauce
1/4 cup lime juice
1 tablespoon tamarind extract
1 teaspoon fermented bean curd

3 tablespoons cilantro, chopped, for garnish
1 tomato, cut into eighths, for garnish
1/4 cup toasted peanuts, chopped, for garnish

For the salad, combine all the vegetables and mix well.

In a separate bowl, combine the dressing ingredients. Pour dressing over vegetables. Add garnishes and mix gently. Taste! Adjust seasonings, palm sugar for sweetness, soy for salt, and lime for tart. Serve immediately.

SMOKED TOFU YUBA WRAPS WITH MUSTARD DIPPING SAUCE

Yuba is also known as tofu skin, a delicacy in Japan for its silky smooth texture and delicate flavor. Very difficult to find fresh unless you have a local tofu maker but easy to find frozen and dried in Asian markets. We always use fresh yuba made a few blocks away by Hodo Soy Beanery.

YIELD: 9 WRAPS

Mustard Dipping Sauce (Karashi):
2 tablespoons dry mustard powder
1 tablespoon soy sauce
1 tablespoon mirin
1 tablespoon water

Whisk ingredients together in a bowl, cover, and let chill at least 30 minutes before serving.

Snow peas:
9 snow peas
1/8 teaspoon baking soda

Prepare the snow peas: De-vein the snow peas by pulling the string from one end to the other, discarding the string. In a stock pot, add 1 quart water and the baking soda and bring to a rapid boil. Drop in snow peas and then immediately take them out, rinsing them under cold water. Set aside.

Marinated, smoked tofu:
1 tablespoon shaoshing wine
2 tablespoons soy sauce
1 teaspoon dark soy sauce
1 tablespoon palm sugar
1 1/4-inch slice ginger
Peel of one orange or tangerine
1/4 cup kombu stock (page 97)
1/8 teaspoon star anise
A few oolong tea leaves
1/2 pound very firm tofu, cut into 1/2-inch slabs

Combine all of the marinade ingredients and mix well. Marinate the sliced tofu for 30 minutes to 4 hours. Remove from marinade and smoke the tofu over applewood for 15 minutes or till nicely browned (see page 137). Be careful not to overdo the smoking part. You can then put the tofu back into the marinade to absorb more flavor.

To assemble the wraps:
1 sheet fresh or frozen yuba (If frozen, thaw completely, first. Dried yuba does not work well for this dish.)

Cut the sheet of yuba into 9 even sections. Place a yuba sheet on your work surface. Place a piece of smoked tofu vertically at the top of the sheet, with a snow pea on top of it. Let a little of both the tofu and snow pea stick out above the top of the yuba sheet. Then wrap up the tofu and snow pea by folding up the bottom of the yuba, and then rolling over one side and then the other side to create a pocket with the contents peeking out of the top. Steam the yuba wraps for 5 minutes before serving.

Garnish with karashi (mustard dipping sauce), or in the spring a cherry mustard, or in summer, a blueberry or peach mustard.

KNISHES

Every culture that has wheat has formed doughs, stuffed them, and either fried, boiled, baked, or steamed them up! The knish is the Ashkenazi version of this wonderful idea. Once upon a time knishes were an Eastern European Jewish street food. For centuries, wooden pushcarts laden with potato and kasha knishes would be found in the shtetls throughout Eastern Europe. In the 20th century, as a huge Jewish migration came to the US, this tradition came to New York City, and today the knish is as much a part of NY food identity as pizza! The last of these pushcart vendors was the legendary Ruby the Knish Man. I was fortunate to grow up in the same neighborhood in which Ruby peddled his wares and he would often be found outside my elementary school (when we were lucky). Ruby, a Hungarian immigrant, was an incredible character, though apparently it was his wife, whom he called "Mom," who was the genius in the kitchen making these knishes. These were the greatest knishes to be found, not to slight the wonderful ones made by my Aunt Rose or to be found at Grabstein's delicatessen, another former Canarsie Jewish culinary institution.

YIELD: ABOUT 20 COCKTAIL KNISHES

Dough:
2 large russet potatoes
1/4 cup olive oil
1 teaspoon salt
1 teaspoon baking powder
1/2 teaspoon turmeric
3 cups flour

Filling:
Roasted Mashed Root Vegetables (page 117)

Peel and chop the potatoes, then steam them for 15 minutes. Mash them. Add the olive oil, salt, baking powder, turmeric, and 3/4 cup water and whisk together. Add flour, slowly incorporating it. Place dough on a board and knead for 10 minutes. Wrap the dough with plastic wrap and refrigerate for at least 1 hour or overnight.

Cut dough into 4 equal parts. Roll each part into a rectangle, 12 inches by 6 inches. Place filling evenly along the long edge of each rectangle. Roll up and pinch the ends to seal. Cut the dough into 2-inch lengths. Fold the dough over the filling on each side to seal the pocket.

Bake at 400°F for 20 minutes or till golden brown.

GRILLED PEACH SALAD WITH CASHEW CHÈVRE ROLLED IN HERBS AND MIZUNA WITH CHERRY-BALSAMIC DRESSING

An improvisation for one of the annual Masumoto Peach dinners that turned into a regular appearance on summer menus.

YIELD: 4 SERVINGS

Dressing:
1/3 cup cherries, pitted
1/4 cup balsamic vinegar
2 tablespoons extra-virgin olive oil
1/4 teaspoon ground coriander
1/2 teaspoon sea salt
Pinch celery seed

4 cups mizuna or arugula
2 ripe peaches
4 balls cashew chèvre rolled in herbs (page 44)

Combine dressing ingredients in a blender. Pour dressing over mizuna and toss and let marinate 1/2 hour.

Heat a grill. Cut peaches in half. Lightly salt the cut side. Grill over coals, cut side down, for 10 minutes or till caramelization begins and nice grill marks appear. Remove skin from peaches.

Divide marinated mizuna among 4 plates. Place a grilled peach on top of the bed of dressed mizuna. Place a chèvre ball in the cavity of each peach.

Option: Garnish with toasted walnuts.

BEET-NUT PÂTÉ

Numerous people have told me this reminds them of steak tartare. Unintentional for certain, as I never ate that dish before becoming vegetarian and I never try to imitate meat! Nonetheless, this is a wonderful spread for fresh bread or a great accompaniment to a buffet spread with other dips, spreads, and salads.

Does not get any easier than this recipe. Throw everything into a food processor and hit the button, that is it!

YIELD: SERVES 4-8

1/2 cup raw cashews
1/2 cup raw almonds
1/2 cup raw pumpkin seeds
1 tablespoon soy sauce
3/4 cup grated beets
1/2 red bell pepper
1/2 small carrot
2-inch piece of daikon
3 green onions, coarsely chopped
1 garlic clove
20 basil leaves

Place everything in the food processor and puree. Add a little bit of water if needed. Season with salt if desired.

HUMMUS SALAD

There are a lot of great hummus recipes and this is my personal favorite. The roasted garlic adds a beautiful creaminess along with the delightful garlicky flavor.

YIELD: SERVES 4-8

1 cup dried garbanzos, soaked overnight, then drained and rinsed
1 bay leaf
1 head garlic
1/3 cup lemon juice
1/2 cup high-quality olive oil
1/3 cup tahini
1 teaspoon cumin
1/2 teaspoon coriander
1/2 teaspoon black pepper
1 teaspoon sea salt
1 cucumber, sliced thin, for garnish
1 carrot, grated, for garnish
1/2 cup alfalfa or radish sprouts, for garnish

Place soaked, rinsed garbanzos in a pot, cover with 1 quart of water and the bay leaf and cover. Bring to a boil, lower heat, and simmer for 45 minutes or till beans are soft. Drain and remove bay leaf.

Meanwhile, roast the head of garlic by placing in a roasting pan, and roast, covered, at 300°F for 2 hours. Remove from oven, and remove cloves from their skins.

In a food processor place the cooked beans, roasted garlic, and the rest of the ingredients except for the garnishes, and puree till very smooth.

Place the hummus in a bowl. Garnish with sliced cucumbers around the sides, grated carrots in the middle, and top with the alfalfa or radish sprouts.

THAI-STYLE CORN FRITTERS WITH PEANUT-CUCUMBER DRESSING

Corn is obviously not native to Southeast Asia. This is an exceptional adaptation to this "foreign" ingredient with Thai flavors.

YIELD: SERVES 4-6

In a saucepan, whisk together the rice vinegar and palm sugar. Over low heat, simmer till it reduces in volume about 25 percent, about 15 minutes. Add peanuts, cucumber, optional ingredients, if using, and a dash of salt and mix well. Chill before serving for optimal flavor. Add cilantro when serving.

Peanut-cucumber dressing:
1/2 cup rice vinegar
1/2 cup palm sugar
1/4 cup roasted peanuts, chopped
1 Japanese cucumber, diced
1 Thai chili chopped, optional
1 shallot, chopped, optional
Sea salt
1 tablespoon chopped cilantro

Lemongrass paste:
1 stalk lemongrass
6 makrut lime leaves (formerly known as kaffir lime)
3 red Thai chilis
1 teaspoon fresh minced ginger
7 cloves garlic
1 teaspoon sea salt
1 tablespoon fermented bean curd

Corn mixture:
4 ears corn, shucked, kernels sliced off the cob
4 green onions, chopped
2 tablespoons cornstarch
2 tablespoons cilantro
2 teaspoons baking soda
1/2 pound silken tofu
1/2-3/4 cup rice flour

Oil for deep-frying

Pound the paste ingredients out in a mortar and pestle or in a food processor. Set aside.

Combine all the ingredients for the corn mixture, and add the lemongrass paste and mix well. This should resemble a cookie dough. Due to the water content of silken tofu varying from brand to brand, the amount of rice flour needed will also vary. Start with a small amount and add more as needed. Since this recipe does not use wheat flour, you do not have to worry about overmixing!

Heat up oil to 375°F. Form fritters into golfball-size pieces, then flatten slightly. Deep-fry in the oil, cooking about 3 minutes on each side or till brown. Turn them only once!

Note: The dough must be used within an hour of making it. Do not refrigerate to use at a later time. Due to the baking soda in the batter, it will draw out water from the vegetables and thus affect the texture if it sits around a long while.

Serve very hot with the peanut-cucumber dressing!

PUMPKIN FRITTERS

A delightful late fall and winter version of the Thai Corn Fritter recipe. Use kabocha, the Japanese pumpkin, for the best results. This is a truly delightful sweet and hot appetizer.

YIELD: SERVES 4-6

Lemongrass paste:

1 stalk lemongrass

6 makrut lime leaves (formerly called kaffir lime)

3 red Thai chilis

1 teaspoon fresh minced ginger

7 cloves garlic

1 teaspoon sea salt

1 tablespoon fermented bean curd

2 cups pumpkin (use kabocha, green Japanese pumpkin), rind on

4 green onions, chopped

2 tablespoon cornstarch

2 tablespoon cilantro

2 teaspoon baking soda

1/2 pound silken tofu

1/2-3/4 cup rice flour

Oil for deep-frying

Pound the paste ingredients out in a mortar and pestle or in a food processor. Set aside.

Dice kabocha (keep rind on!!) into 1/4-inch pieces, the size of corn kernels. If the kabocha is too large, it will not cook evenly.

Combine paste with the pumpkin, green onions, cornstarch, cilantro, baking soda, silken tofu, and rice flour and mix well. This should resemble cookie dough. Due to the water content of silken tofu varying from brand to brand, the amount of rice flour needed will also vary. Start with a small amount and add more as needed. Since this recipe does not use wheat flour, you do not have to worry about overmixing!

Heat up oil to 375°F. Form fritters into small golfball-size pieces, then flatten slightly. Deep-fry in hot oil and cook about 3 minutes on each side or till brown. Turn only once!

Note: The dough must be used within an hour of making it. Do not refrigerate to use at a later time. Due to the baking soda in the batter, it will draw out water from the vegetables and thus affect the texture if it sits around a long while.

SOCCA WITH SMOKED EGGPLANT DIP & JULIENNED VEGETABLES

This chickpea flatbread from Southern France is one of the most popular finger foods on my catering menus. We serve this at practically every catering event, varying the toppings based on the season. The combination of the hot crisp crêpe with the different textured toppings is always a hit with any audience.

This is best cooked in a cast iron pan or a crêpe pan. Keep the batter thin for best texture and flavor. If baked, make them a maximum of 1/8 inch thick.

YIELD: ABOUT 1 DOZEN CRÉPES

2 cups chickpea flour
2 cups water
1/4 cup olive oil, plus more for coating the pan
2 teaspoons sea salt
1 tablespoon dried sage
1 tablespoon dried rosemary
1/2 teaspoon black pepper

In a bowl, whisk together all the ingredients. Cover and let rest for 2 hours.

Over medium heat, warm up the cast iron pan or crêpe pan for 10 minutes. Coat the pan with olive oil. Whisk the chickpea flour mixture well and then ladle about 1/3 cup of the mixture in the center, making a circle, extending outwards till the batter thinly coats the crêpe pan. Cook over medium heat till it starts to bubble. Turn only once and cook on the other side for about 1 minute.

Remove from pan, cut into 4-8 sections, like a pizza, and cover with toppings. Best served hot and crisp!

Toppings:
1 tablespoon olive oil
1/4 red onion, cut into half moons
1 carrot, julienned
10 snow peas, julienned
10 pieces asparagus, julienned
1/2 teaspoon sea salt
Dash black pepper
1/4 teaspoon red pepper flakes
2 tablespoons pine nuts
2 teaspoons lemon juice

Always use what is in season! For spring I like to julienne asparagus, snow peas, carrots, and red onions, and do the following:

In a hot skillet, add olive oil. Add red onion, carrot, snow peas, and asparagus and sauté for 3 minutes. Add sea salt, black pepper, red pepper flakes, and pine nuts and sauté for 2 more minutes. Add lemon juice and mix well.

In summer, replace the asparagus with the kernels cut from 2 ears of corn, for great texture! In fall and winter, replace asparagus with thinly julienned kabocha or cubes of butternut squash.

Dot the socca with the prepared vegetables and serve hot or warm. This can also work at room temperature.

Note: In summer, I always put Smoked Eggplant Dip (page 70) on socca and then add the vegetables on top of the dip. In winter, I add a bean dip and place the vegetables on top of the dip.

SMOKED EGGPLANT DIP

Smoking takes eggplants to a whole new level! Smoking is a primal flavor, perhaps the second flavor humans got used to after raw. I never miss meat foods but once I started smoking tempeh, tofu, and vegetables, I realized how much I missed smoked flavors! Outdoor grills are ideal for smoking foods. Stovetop smokers are available for inside the home or you can easily rig a smoker up, using a wok, chopsticks, and a wok lid.

YIELD: SERVES 8

2 large eggplants
Olive oil
Sea salt

1/2 cup raw walnuts
2 cloves garlic
1/4 cup lemon juice
1 teaspoon salt
1 teaspoon cumin
1 teaspoon paprika
1 tomato, chopped
1/2 teaspoon black pepper

Rub a little olive oil and salt on the 2 eggplants, keeping the eggplants whole, with the stems on the cap intact. Smoke the eggplants using applewood or alder or a combination, till the eggplants totally collapse. Remove the charred skin

Place walnuts in a hot cast iron frying pan. Over low heat, toast them lightly till they are aromatic, about 5 minutes. Place the flesh of the eggplants and toasted walnuts along with the rest of the ingredients in a food processor and puree till smooth.

SPRING ROLLS

A classic appetizer from Southeast Asia. I have access to local, daily-made rice noodles in Oakland's Chinatown. If you live near large Asian or Asian-American populations you can probably find the same, otherwise use dried rice noodles. This dish is all about a combination of textures along with extremely fresh herbs. There is little technique in this dish, thus it is all about the quality and freshness of ingredients.

You need a variety of fresh herbs. Again, if you live near a large Asian population you may have access to Chinese hot mint, shiso, Thai basil, opal basil, cilantro, mint, basil, ram, and Chinese shiso. Use at least one basil, cilantro, and at least one mint. The greater the variety of herbs, the more your mouth and senses will be delighted! Simply cleaning and pulling leaves off stems will be a wonderful aromatherapy experience.

YIELD: 4 ROLLS

1/4 pound fresh rice noodles
4 rice-paper spring roll wrappers
1/4 pound tempeh, sliced 1/8 inch thick, deep-fried until golden brown (page 134)
1 cup various fresh herbs (see note, above), removed from stems, cleaned and dried

Soak the rice noodles in hot water till soft. Do not boil rice noodles. For best texture pour boiling water over the noodles and let them soak for 1-4 minutes till they are soft. Check regularly so as not to oversoak! Rinse in cold water to stop the cooking process and remove the starches. You can do this ahead of time, and to revitalize the noodles, simply rinse them in water again and then thoroughly drain.

To assemble the rolls, drop the rice paper in cool water for a few seconds. Depending on the brand, some have to soak longer than others. You want the rice paper to be malleable or it will tear apart when rolling. Drip dry. Place on a cutting board. On the end closest to you, place some rice noodles. Put 2 slices of tempeh on top of the noodles. Add herbs on top of tempeh. Roll up like a burrito; first fold up. Then fold over from each side. Then roll upwards and press lightly to seal. Serve immediately for best texture! The hot crisp tempeh next to the chewy noodles and the crisp herbs is a sensation with universal appeal.

Serve with Peanut Sauce (page 34), tamarind sauce (page 35), chili oil (page 36), or sweet and sour peach sauce (page 32).

SOPES

Sopes are an amazing appetizer, layered with flavors and textures. Sopes are one of the many ways to make and shape homemade tortillas. These are a common street food in Mexico City as well as an antojito, or small dish, found in many restaurants.

YIELD: 30 SOPES

PART 1: HOMEMADE TORTILLAS

YIELD: ABOUT 2 1/2 DOZEN TORTILLAS

3 1/2 cups masa
1 teaspoon sea salt
2 1/4 cups water
Oil for deep-frying

Combine masa and salt. Add the water and knead until smooth. Cover tightly with plastic wrap and let sit 30 minutes. Divide dough into 30 balls. Flatten each ball with a tortilla press. Preheat a skillet, griddle, or cast iron pan. Do not oil the skillet! Cook each tortilla for 1 minute on 1 side. Then turn and cook for 1 more minute on the other side.

While tortilla is hot, press the sides inward to form a wall, thus creating a bowl out of the tortilla. This is difficult as the tortilla is hot and your fingers will easily burn. However, it must be done quickly after the tortilla comes off the griddle or it will break apart when manipulated after it cools off. This takes practice, obviously! The more experienced you are in the kitchen, the easier your fingers can handle the heat of the tortillas.

Right before serving, deep-fry each bowl till golden brown. Immediately serve with the three fillings.

PART 2: MANGO SALSA

2 ripe Manila mangos, peeled and seeded and
   diced into 1/4-inch cubes
1 green chile, serrano or jalapeño, seeded, minced
1/4 cup red onion, diced
2 tablespoons cilantro, minced
1/2 teaspoon sea salt
2 limes, juiced

Combine all ingredients in a bowl and mix well.

Note: Add more chilis if you desire more heat.

PART 3: BLACK BEAN PUREE

2 cups dried black beans
1 bay leaf
2 teaspoons olive oil
1 onion, chopped
3 teaspoons sea salt
1 carrot, chopped
1 red pepper, chopped
2 jalapeños, minced
5 cloves garlic, minced
2 teaspoons cumin
2 teaspoons oregano
1 teaspoon ancho chile powder
1 teaspoon sweet paprika
1 teaspoon pasilla chile powder
1 teaspoon marjoram
3 tablespoons lime juice
1/4 cup fresh epazote
2 tablespoons cilantro
3 tablespoons extra-virgin olive oil

Start the day before: Soak beans overnight, then rinse and drain. Place in a pot with 2 quarts water and the bay leaf. Bring to a boil, cover, lower heat, and let simmer, 1/2 hour or till beans are cooked. Remove bay leaf and drain beans, then set aside.

In a skillet, warm up the olive oil. Add onions and salt and over medium heat, cook for 10 minutes, stirring occasionally. Add carrots, peppers, garlic, cumin, oregano, ancho chile powder, sweet paprika, pasilla chile powder, and marjoram and continue cooking for 10 more minutes. Add a little water if necessary to keep from sticking.

Place the cooked vegetable mixture with the cooked beans in a food processor and puree. Add the lime juice, epazote, and cilantro and puree. With the machine running, pour in the 3 tablespoons extra-virgin olive oil to the puree. Season with more lime or salt if needed.

PART 4: GUACAMOLE

2 large ripe avocados
3 tablespoons lime juice
1/2 teaspoon sea salt
1/2 teaspoon cumin
1/4 teaspoon coriander
1/2 teaspoon chopped green chili (serrano is good), optional
1 green onion, chopped
1 tablespoon cilantro, chopped

With a fork, mash your avocados in a bowl. Add the rest of ingredients and mix well.

Season with more lime and/or salt if needed.

Assembling the sopes: Fry the tortilla bowls and then top with bean puree, guacamole, and mango salsa and serve fresh!

BREADS & GRAINS

BAGELS

Bagels are one of my comfort foods. Having grown up in Brooklyn of Jewish heritage, I often wake up on Sunday mornings craving a hot bagel. While in college and grad school in Florida this became a problem as there were no decent bagel shops to be found. Thus I learned to make my own! Finding great bagels outside of New York City and Montreal can be a real challenge. And no, it is not simply the water that is the problem, though the very soft water found in New York City sure does help make great bread!

YIELD: 1 DOZEN BAGELS

1 teaspoon active dry yeast
4 tablespoons rice malt, barley malt, or agave
2 cups warm water (105°F)
1 teaspoon sea salt
2 cups whole-wheat flour
About 3 cups white flour
1 tablespoon olive oil
1 1/2 teaspoons baking soda
Dried garlic, dried onion, sesame seeds, poppy seeds, coarse salt, for garnish (optional)

In a bowl, add yeast, 1 tablespoon malt, and the water. Let yeast proof till the surface becomes foamy, about 5 minutes. Whisk in the salt. With a wooden spoon add the whole-wheat flour and 2 cups white flour, stirring until incorporated.

Place the dough on a sturdy, clean surface and slowly work in the rest of the white flour. Knead for 10 minutes or till dough is smooth. Coat the dough with the olive oil, place in a bowl, and cover tightly with a clean dish towel.

Let rise till doubled in size, about 1 hour, though the time may vary greatly due to temperature and altitude.

After dough doubles, knead it lightly for 1 minute. Divide dough into 12 equal parts. Round each of the 12 pieces of dough, by rolling them each gently in your palm against your kneading surface. If needed, lightly flour your palm but do not flour the work surface. The result of rounding will create a small hole or indentation on the bottom of the "roll" when you are done. With your thumb, press into and through the center to make a bagel shape.

Place on a floured surface, cover with a clean kitchen towel, and let rise till doubled, about 1 hour. As before, this time will vary depending on temperature and altitude.

Meanwhile, preheat your oven to 500°F or its highest setting and place a baking stone in the oven. In a large pan or pot, bring 3 quarts of water to a boil and add the baking soda and 3 tablespoons malt. The baking soda is necessary to get the bagels to brown. The change of pH to a more base level, caused by the addition of baking soda to the boiling water, is necessary for bagel baking (and pretzel baking!).

After the bagels finish their second rise, boil each bagel for 1 minute on each side. Boil 1 minute, turn, boil another minute. Keep the water at a rapid boil!

Now your bagels are ready to bake. If you want you can coat them with any of the following: dried garlic, dried onion, sesame seeds, poppy seeds, coarse salt.

Bake on the hot baking stone at 500°F for about 15 minutes.

The bagels are best served within 15 minutes of coming out of the oven!

BIALYS

Another one of my very favorite breads! These are a little work to produce but well worth the effort. This is a very wet dough which is nearly impossible to produce by hand, thus the need for a stand mixer or food processor.

A bialy is an onion-filled bread, brought to the United States by Polish and other Eastern European Jewish immigrants. Often found in bagel shops in New York City, they are one of the great breads of the world.

YIELD: 1 DOZEN BIALYS

1 tablespoon olive oil
2 large onions, diced
2 1/4 teaspoons sea salt
2 tablespoons poppy seeds
1 3/4 cups warm water (105° F)
1 1/2 teaspoons active dry yeast
1/2 teaspoon rice malt, barley malt, or agave
1 cup whole-wheat flour
3 cups white flour

In a frying pan, heat the olive oil. Add onion and 1/4 teaspoon salt. Over low flame, covered, cook onion for 30 minutes, stirring occasionally, till very caramelized. Remove cover, add poppy seeds, stir, and set aside.

In a bowl, add water, yeast and the malt. Let proof till foamy, about 5 minutes. Add 2 teaspoons sea salt and whisk well. Add flours, one cup at a time, at first mixing with a spoon and then putting the dough into a food processor or stand mixer to finish kneading. Let knead about 20 minutes! Do not add flour to make it a dry dough. Place dough in a large bowl and cover tightly with plastic wrap. Let dough double in size, about 2 hours.

Divide the onion-poppy seed filling into 12 parts. Flour hands to work with the dough in the next step. Divide dough into 12 parts. Place a baking stone in your oven and preheat to 500°F or the highest setting. Round each of the 12 pieces of dough, by rolling them gently in your palm against your kneading surface. If needed, lightly flour your palm but do not flour the work surface. The result of rounding will create a small hole or indentation on the bottom of the "roll" when you are done. Stretch each rounded piece of dough into a small circle about 6 inches in diameter. Stretch the center thinner than the edges. Place some of the onion-poppy seed filling on each dough's center.

Bake about 11 minutes or till lightly browned.

ONION PUMPERNICKEL BREAD

A favorite since childhood.

YIELD: 2 LOAVES

1 cup stout or doppelbock beer
1/2 cup black coffee
1/4 cup blackstrap molasses
2 teaspoons active dry yeast
2 tablespoons cocoa powder
2 teaspoons sea salt
2 cups rye flour
3 cups white flour
1 tablespoon olive oil
1 onion, minced

In a bowl, add stout, coffee, 1/2 cup water, molasses, and yeast and whisk together. Let the mixture get foamy, about 5 minutes. Add cocoa powder and sea salt and whisk together. Add rye flour and mix well. Place dough on a clean surface and slowly incorporate the white flour. Knead well for 20 minutes or till very smooth. Coat with the olive oil and let sit 2 hours, covered tightly, or till doubled in size. There will be variation in rising time depending on temperature and altitude.

Place a baking stone in the oven and preheat to 500°F.

Add onion to the dough and knead 2 minutes. Divide into 2 equal parts and shape into round loaves. Bake for 25 minutes or till done. Test with a knife in the center of the dough; it is done when the knife comes out totally clean with no residue on the surface.

ANADAMA BREAD

A favorite of mine since college days. This bread is from the time when English settlers contacted (being nice here) Native Americans in the northeast United States. The combination of corn and wheat is a wonderful early culinary fusion that developed from a not always nice contact between cultures.

YIELD: 2 LOAVES

1 cup warm soy milk (almond or rice can work as well) (105° F)
1 cup warm water (105° F)
1 teaspoon active dry yeast
2 tablespoons blackstrap molasses
2 teaspoons sea salt
1 cup cornmeal
1 cup whole-wheat flour
2 cups white flour
2 tablespoons olive oil

In a bowl, add soy milk, water, yeast, and molasses and whisk together. Let the mixture get foamy, about 5 minutes. Add salt and cornmeal to the yeast mixture and whisk together. Add whole-wheat flour and mix together with a wooden spoon. Place on a kneading surface and incorporate the white flour, kneading it in. Add more flour if needed and knead at least 10 minutes or till you have a very smooth dough. Cover dough with the olive oil, place in bowl, and cover tightly with a clean kitchen towel. Let rise till doubled, about an hour; time may vary due to temperature and altitude.

After dough rises, knead again for 1 minute. Cut dough in half and shape into 2 rounds. Place on floured surface and cover with a towel and let double in size, about 1 hour. Like before, time will vary depending on temperature and altitude.

Preheat oven to 500°F or its highest setting and place a baking stone in the oven. Bake the 2 loaves for about 25 minutes or till done in the center. Test with a knife in the center of the dough; it is done when the knife comes out totally clean with no residue on the surface.

PITA BREAD

YIELD: 1 DOZEN PITA BREADS

2 cups warm water (105° F)
1 teaspoon maple syrup or agave
2 teaspoons active dry yeast
2 teaspoons sea salt
2 cups whole-wheat flour
2 1/2 cups white flour
2 tablespoons olive oil

In a bowl, add water, maple syrup, and yeast, whisking together. Let the mixture get foamy, about 5 minutes. Whisk in the salt. Stir in the whole-wheat flour. Put dough on a large kneading board and slowly incorporate the white flour. Knead 10 minutes or till very smooth. Place dough in a large bowl. Cover dough with the olive oil, cover bowl tightly, and let rise till doubled, about 1 hour. There will be variation in time, depending on temperature and altitude.

Place baking stone in the oven and preheat to 500°F. Punch dough down, then lightly knead for 1 minute. Divide dough into 12 parts. Round each of the 12 pieces of dough, by rolling them gently in your palm against your kneading surface. If needed, lightly flour your palm but do not flour the work surface. Press down to a circle and roll out to about 6 inches in diameter. Cover the dough and let rise till doubled, about 40 minutes.

Place breads on the baking stone and bake for 7 minutes, turn them over, and bake another 5 minutes.

MULTIGRAIN SEED AND HERB ROLLS

YIELD: 12-15 ROLLS

2 teaspoons active dry yeast

2 cups warm water (105° F)

2 teaspoons blackstrap molasses

2 teaspoons sea salt

1/3 cup buckwheat flour

1/3 cup oat flour

1/3 cup cornmeal

1/3 cup rye flour

1/3 cup rice flour

2 1/2 cups white flour

2 tablespoons olive oil

3 tablespoons poppy seeds

3 tablespoons sunflower seeds

3 tablespoons pumpkin seeds

3 tablespoons sesame seeds

2 teaspoons dried sage

2 teaspoons dried rosemary

In a bowl, dissolve yeast with water and molasses. Let the mixture get foamy, about 5 minutes. Whisk in the salt. Add each flour, one at a time, except for the white flour, incorporating each fully before adding the next. Turn the batter onto a kneading board. Slowly add the white flour, kneading about 20 minutes. Cover dough with the olive oil, place in a bowl, cover tightly, and let rise 90 minutes or till doubled. Rising time may vary based on temperature and altitude.

Punch dough down and add the seeds and herbs to the dough. Knead 2 minutes to incorporate it all together. Divide dough into 12-15 pieces. Round each piece of dough by rolling it gently in your palm against your kneading surface. If needed, lightly flour your palm but do not flour the work surface. Place each rounded piece on a well floured board. Cover with a towel and let rise about 45 minutes or till doubled in size. As before, there may be variation in rising time due to temperature and altitude.

Place a baking stone in the oven and preheat to 500°F or the highest possible temperature. Place the risen rolls on the baking stone, 2 inches apart. Bake for 20 minutes or until they test done.

Test with a knife in the center of the dough; it is done when the knife comes out totally clean with no residue on the surface.

PERSIAN BASMATI PILAF

An incredibly flavorful dish that I learned from a friend from Iran while in grad school.

YIELD: 8 SERVINGS

2 cups brown basmati rice
4 tablespoons sea salt
4 tablespoons olive oil
1/2 cup chopped dill
1/2 cup chopped cilantro
1/2 cup chopped parsley
1/2 cup chopped green onions

The night before you wish to cook the dish, place the basmati rice and 2 tablespoons sea salt into a pot with 2 quarts of water and let soak for 8-14 hours. Thoroughly rinse the rice and drain.

Bring 2 quarts of fresh water to a boil. Add the soaked, drained rice and the remaining 2 tablespoons salt to the water. Return to a boil and cook for 15 minutes over medium heat, uncovered. Pour rice through a sieve to drain the water. Rinse the rice well and drain again.

Heat the oven to 350°F. Coat the bottom and sides of a cast iron pot with 2 tablespoons olive oil. Add half of the rice to the pot. Top the rice with the herbs and green onions. Top the herbs with the rest of the rice and drizzle the remaining 2 tablespoons of olive oil over the rice. Cover very tightly with aluminum foil. Bake for one hour.

WILD RICE PILAF

YIELD: 4-6 SERVINGS

1/2 cup wild rice
1/2 cup brown basmati rice
Sea salt
2 tablespoons olive oil
1 onion, diced
1 stalk celery, diced
1 carrot, diced
2 tablespoons dry white wine
Black pepper
3 tablespoons parsley, chopped

In a rice cooker, cook the wild rice and basmati rice with 1/2 teaspoon sea salt. Set aside.

In a hot frying pan, add olive oil, onion, and 1/2 teaspoon salt and cook for 10 minutes over low heat, stirring occasionally. Add celery and carrot and cook 3 more minutes. Add wine and cook 1 minute more. Add black pepper to taste, and the parsley. Add this mixture to the cooked rice and combine gently.

Optional: Add 2 tablespoons dried unsweetened cranberries and 2 tablespoons toasted pine nuts.

HOMEMADE NOODLES

A basic noodle recipe to play with.

YIELD: 1 POUND NOODLES

2 cups semolina flour
1/2 teaspoon sea salt

Combine flour and salt. Add 1/2 cup plus 2 tablespoons water and knead on a work surface for 15 minutes. Wrap tightly in plastic wrap and let rest 1 hour.

Roll out dough with a rolling pin or pasta machine to make sheets and then cut to desired size for noodles or dumplings. Drop noodles in boiling water and cook 1 minute or until al dente.

HOMEMADE RAMEN NOODLES

Ramen is a very special noodle! Originally from China, it was imported to Japan where a huge culinary culture exists around this amazing noodle. In the area of China where ramen originated, the local spring water is very alkaline. This produces a firmer noodle with a different color and texture than if the pH of the water was normal. To emulate this at home, we use baking soda to change the pH to a more base level.

To use the baking soda, we first want to "burn" it. Lay the baking soda on a baking tray and bake for 1 hour at 250°F.

YIELD: 1 POUND NOODLES

2 cups flour
1/2 teaspoon salt
1/2 teaspoon "burnt" baking soda

Combine flour, salt, and baking soda. Add 3/4 cup water and knead till very smooth and elastic.

Wrap dough tightly in plastic wrap and refrigerate dough overnight.

Bring dough to room temperature. Give it a second kneading for 10 minutes. Wrap tightly and let rest 1 hour.

Roll dough out and cut into noodles. Drop noodles into boiling water and cook for 1 minute or till al dente.

HOMEMADE SOBA NOODLES

The key to soba is using the right kind of buckwheat flour. One must use soba-ko, found in some Japanese markets. The buckwheat flour we usually use for pancakes and waffles is too gritty and does not work for soba! Or you can grind your own buckwheat flour finely in a grain mill.

YIELD: 1 POUND NOODLES

1 cup soba-ko (see note)
1 cup white flour
1/2 teaspoon sea salt
1 tablespoon grated yama-imo (see note)

Combine flours and salt. Add 1/2 cup plus 2 tablespoons water and yama-imo and knead for at least 20 minutes on a flat surface. Soba takes a great deal of kneading to create noodles that do not fall apart. Wrap dough well and let rest 1 hour.

Roll dough out thinly with a rolling pin or pasta machine and cut to desired thickness and length.

Notes: Yama-imo is a Japanese mountain potato and found in Japanese markets and some Asian markets. When grated, it resembles egg whites in appearance as well as in the way it helps to bind.

Soba-ko is Japanese buckwheat flour, different from the typical buckwheat flour used for pancakes and crepes. Soba-ko is finer and lighter. Nijiya Market is an excellent mail order source if you do not have Japanese markets near where you live and cook.

Variation: Homemade Green Tea Soba Noodles

Add 1 tablespoon matcha to the above recipe and omit 1 tablespoon white flour.

PUMPKIN GNOCCHI

A fall and winter favorite.

YIELD: 4-8 SERVINGS

1 cup roasted pureed pumpkin
1 teaspoon sea salt
1/4 teaspoon nutmeg
1 1/2 cups semolina flour

Combine pumpkin with salt and nutmeg and mix well. Slowly incorporate the flour till you have a dough. The less flour you add, the lighter the dumplings will result! The amount of flour needed will vary greatly depending on the moisture of the roasted pumpkin. Let dough rest, covered, for 1/2 hour.

Cut dough into 4 parts. Roll each part out into a 3/4-inch-thick log. Cut logs into 1-inch lengths. Drop the dumplings into boiling water. When they float, they are finished. Remove from the water, drain, and sauce immediately.

My favorite way to serve this is with Walnut-Sage sauce (page 49).

COLD NOODLES WITH SESAME SAUCE

This Sichuan dish is one of my favorite hot weather dishes! Spicy, ice-cold noodles with sliced cucumbers are a refreshing and relaxing way to lower your body temperature in midsummer.

YIELD: 2 SERVINGS

Sauce:
1/2 cup kombu stock (page 97)
1/4 cup roasted peanuts
1/4 cup toasted sesame seeds
1 fresh green chile
2 teaspoons minced garlic
1 teaspoon minced ginger
1/2 teaspoon Sichuan peppercorns
1/4 cup soy sauce
1/4 cup palm sugar
2 teaspoons chinkiang vinegar
1 tablespoon rice vinegar
1 tablespoon cilantro
1 tablespoon Sichuan chili oil (page 36)

1/2 recipe of Homemade Noodle dough, cut into spaghetti size
1 cucumber, slivered, for garnish

Prepare the sauce: In a blender, add all sauce ingredients and blend till smooth. Chill.

Bring 2 quarts of water to a rapid boil. Drop in noodles and cook 60 seconds or till al dente. Drain and rinse with cold water. Place noodles in bowl, garnish with cucumber, and pour sauce over them.

COLD SOBA NOODLES WITH SOY-SESAME MILK (KON GOOK SOO)

Thank you to one of my favorite restaurants, Pyong Chong Tofu house in Oakland, for introducing me to this wonderful summer dish. This is another amazing, refreshing summer cold noodle dish, this one from Korea. Simple to make and incredibly delightful results.

YIELD: 2 SERVINGS

1/2 cup dried soybeans, soaked overnight, rinsed and drained

2 tablespoons raw sesame seeds, soaked overnight, rinsed and drained

2 tablespoons raw almonds, soaked overnight, rinsed and drained

3 cups cold water

1/2 teaspoon sea salt, plus more to taste

1/2 teaspoon white pepper

1/2 recipe Homemade Soba Noodles (page 87)

1 cucumber, julienned

Ice

Cook soybeans in 1 quart of boiling water for 40 minutes or till soft. Rinse and drain. Place soybeans in a bowl, then fill with water. Using a massaging motion, rub the beans till they split and the hulls come off. The hulls will float and can be discarded. Remove about 90% of the hulls.

Add the dehulled soybeans to a blender and add the soaked and drained sesame seeds and almonds to the blender with the cold water. Puree on high speed for 2 minutes and then chill this mixture till very cold. Add the sea salt and white pepper to the soy milk mixture and blend well.

Cook soba noodles in boiling water for 1 minute or till al dente. Rinse noodles with cold water. Divide the noodles between 2 bowls. Add a few pieces of ice to the bowls and top the noodles with julienned cucumber. Pour the soy-sesame milk over the noodles. Sprinkle bowls with salt or let the diners salt to their own desire. Serve immediately.

HOMEMADE FETTUCCINE WITH CREAM SAUCE

My take on the classic Italian dish.

YIELD: 2 SERVINGS

Cashew cream:
1/3 cup raw unsalted cashews

2 tablespoons olive oil
3 cloves garlic, minced
1 cup fresh peas
2 cups mushrooms, sliced (see note)
1 1/2 teaspoons sea salt
1 teaspoon freshly cracked black pepper
1/4 cup Marsala wine
1/4 cup basil, chopped
1/2 recipe Homemade Noodle dough (page 84), cut to fettuccine size

In a blender, combine cashews and 1 cup water and puree on high for 2 minutes, set aside.

In a hot frying pan, add olive oil and garlic and sauté for 30 seconds. Add peas and mushrooms and continue sautéing 5 minutes. Add salt, pepper, and Marsala wine and cook 2 minutes. Add cashew cream, cook till the mixture slightly thickens, adding more water if it is too thick. Add basil and stir gently. Season to taste with more salt and pepper if needed.

Add noodles to rapidly boiling water. Cook for 60 seconds or till al dente. Drain the noodles, place them on a plate, and pour the sauce over them. Serve HOT!

Note: White or crimini mushrooms can be used; however, wild mushrooms have far more flavor. Morels or chanterelles are excellent when in season and available!

WILD MUSHROOM/CHEESE RAVIOLI

YIELD: 4 SERVINGS

1 pound wild mushrooms (Chanterelles or morels are my favorites for this!)
1/2 teaspoon sea salt
1/2 teaspoon black pepper
1/4 cup parsley, minced
1/2 recipe Almond Ricotta (page 45)

1 recipe fresh Homemade Noodle dough (page 84), divided into 4 parts

Clean mushrooms very well and chop into very small pieces. Heat a frying pan over medium heat and add chopped mushrooms. Stirring occasionally, dry fry the mushrooms till they release their water. Remove from heat and drain very well. Season the mushrooms with the sea salt, black pepper, and parsley. Combine the mushroom mixture with the almond ricotta and mix well.

For simplicity, use a ravioli mold! These are easily found at any kitchen supply place and are inexpensive. Roll out each piece of noodle dough till thin: On most pasta rollers, I go down to the 5th setting for ravioli. Spread the dough over the ravioli mold. Add a small spoonful of filling to each ravioli pocket. Cover with another layer of dough, using a rolling pin to go over the top to remove air pockets. Cut carefully.

Add ravioli to rapidly boiling water. When they float, they are finished. Remove and serve immediately with pesto sauce (page 44).

STEAMED DUMPLINGS FILLED WITH TEMPEH CHAR SIU

I absolutely love Chinese food and can never stop eating it and trying to learn new dishes to prepare.

YIELD: 8 SERVINGS

1 teaspoon sesame oil
2 cups soybean sprouts, cut into 1/2-inch pieces
5 green onions, chopped
1 recipe Tempeh Char Siu (page 140)
1 recipe Homemade Noodle dough (page 84)

In a hot wok, add the oil, bean sprouts, and green onions and stir fry 2 minutes. Add this to the tempeh char siu and mix well.

For simple rolling, use a ravioli mold! Roll out noodle dough very thin; I use the 5th setting on a pasta roller. Place a sheet of dough over the ravioli mold. Fill each depression of the mold with 2 tablespoons tempeh char siu mixture. Place another sheet of dough over the mold and roll flat. Cut each dumpling out. You can then shape these by folding the sides over.

Steam dumplings for 15 minutes and serve with Chinese-style mustard (page 53) or chili oil (page 36).

BUCKWHEAT WAFFLES

A simple recipe that will always impress.

YIELD: 3 LARGE WAFFLES

Dry mix:
1/2 cup buckwheat flour
1/2 cup white flour
1 tablespoon palm sugar
1/4 teaspoon baking soda
1/2 teaspoon baking powder

Wet mix:
1 teaspoon vanilla extract
1 tablespoon grapeseed oil
1 cup soy milk (almond milk or rice milk can work as well)

Heat a waffle iron. In one bowl whisk together the dry
mix. In another bowl, whisk together the wet mix. Add
wet to dry, stir gently, leaving some lumps. Add 2/3 cup
of mix to the oiled waffle iron and cook till done.

CORN AND RYE SAVORY WAFFLES

A savory waffle, great with brunch. Serve a scramble on top of it.

YIELD: 4 LARGE WAFFLES

Dry mix:
1 cup rye flour
1 cup cornmeal
1/2 teaspoon sea salt
1 teaspoon baking powder
1/2 teaspoon baking soda

Wet mix:
2 tablespoons grapeseed oil
2 cups soy milk (almond milk or rice milk can work as well)

Heat a waffle iron. In one bowl, whisk together the dry ingredients. In a separate bowl, whisk together the wet ingredients.

Add wet to dry, stirring gently, leaving some lumps. Pour 3/4 cup batter into the oiled waffle iron and cook till done.

Serve with tempeh scramble (pages 134-136)!

SOUPS & STOCKS

KOMBU STOCK

YIELD: 1 1/2 QUARTS

3 dried shiitake mushrooms
1 6-inch-square piece kombu

In a small stockpot, place mushrooms, kombu, and 2 quarts water. Bring to boil, cover, lower heat, and let simmer 30 minutes.

BASIC VEGETABLE STOCK

YIELD: 1 1/2 QUARTS

1 6-inch-square piece kombu
3 dried shiitake mushrooms
2 button mushrooms
1 yellow onion, quartered
1 stalk celery
1 carrot
1 teaspoon black peppercorns
1 sprig thyme
1 sprig oregano
1 sprig rosemary

Place all ingredients in a pot with 2 quarts water and bring to a boil. Cover, lower heat, and simmer 2 or more hours. Drain stock through cheesecloth to remove all solids.

SOUTHEAST ASIAN STOCK

YIELD: 1 1/2 QUARTS

1 6-inch-square piece kombu

3 dried shiitake mushrooms

1 clove

1 small piece star anise (do not use a whole piece, only 1 small part, or it will be too strong)

1 carrot

5 cloves garlic

1 stalk celery

1 yellow onion, quartered

1 stalk lemongrass, cut into 1-inch pieces

5 makrut lime leaves (formerly known as kaffir lime)

1 teaspoon coriander seeds

1 teaspoon black peppercorns

Add all ingredients to a stock pot with 2 quarts water. Bring to
a boil, cover, lower heat, and let simmer 1 hour or longer. Drain
stock through cheesecloth to remove all solids.

SICHUAN TOFU WATERCRESS SOUP

YIELD: 4 SERVINGS

1 tablespoon sesame oil (not toasted!)

1 slice ginger, 1/4 inch thick by 1 inch long

4 dried tien tsen chilis, kept whole

1/2 teaspoon Sichuan peppercorns, mashed in a mortar and pestle

4 cloves garlic, chopped

2 tablespoons palm sugar

1/4 cup soy sauce

1 bunch watercress, chopped (spinach can work and basil can also be substituted for a very different result)

4 cups Kombu Stock (page 97)

8 ounces medium tofu, cut into 1/2-inch cubes

2 teaspoons chinkiang vinegar

2 green onions, chopped

Heat up a wok and add sesame oil, ginger, chilis, peppercorns, and garlic and stir-fry 30 seconds.
Add palm sugar and soy sauce and stir-fry 2 minutes. Add watercress, stock, and tofu and bring to simmer.
Add vinegar and green onions. Season to taste; more soy sauce if salt is needed, more vinegar if more tart is needed. Remove ginger slice and dried chilis before serving.

Options: Replace watercress with 1-2 cups of any of the following greens, chopped, for a similar yet very different soup: spinach, choy sum, basil, collards, cilantro.

SIMPLE MUNG DAL SOUP

I LOVE this soup!! This has been an every-week dish in my home for many years. So simple to make with such delightful results in texture and flavor. Years ago, I asked some friends from India what they considered the best way to start learning about Indian food, and they always said to start with dal. So here is the first Indian dish I learned, and still one of my favorite dishes from this rich culinary tradition.

YIELD: 4-6 SERVINGS

2 tablespoons coconut oil

2/3 cup dried whole or split mung beans

1 tablespoon fresh ginger, minced

1 fresh green chili, minced

2 teaspoons coriander powder

1 teaspoon cumin seeds

1 teaspoon brown mustard seeds

1 1/2 teaspoons salt

1/4 teaspoon asafoetida

3 tablespoons cilantro, chopped

In a soup pot bring 6 cups water to boil. Add 1/2 tablespoon coconut oil, mung beans, ginger, chili, and coriander. Bring to a simmer, cover, lower heat, and cook for 1 hour and 15 minutes.

In a hot frying pan or wok, add the remaining 1 1/2 tablespoons coconut oil. Add cumin seeds and mustard seeds and stir fry for 30 seconds. Add this to the cooked beans. Add salt, asafoetida, and cilantro, and whisk together. Cover for 1 minute and then serve hot.

Variation: Dal with tomato soup

Another easy variation for summer and fall. Add 4 chopped heirloom tomatoes and 2 teaspoons garam marsala at the beginning.

LENTIL SOUP

There is nothing quite as comforting as a hot bowl of lentil soup. There are countless recipes to make exceptional soups. Use your imagination to come up with your own flavor combinations.

YIELD: 4-6 SERVINGS

1 cup green lentils, soaked overnight, rinsed and drained
1 bay leaf
3 tablespoons olive oil
1 onion, diced
1 1/2 teaspoons sea salt
1 carrot, diced
1 parsnip root, diced
1 small celery root, peeled and diced
1 stalk celery, diced
10 cloves garlic, minced
1 teaspoon oregano
1 teaspoon marjoram
1 teaspoon rosemary
1 teaspoon thyme
1 teaspoon sweet paprika
1 teaspoon smoked paprika
Freshly cracked black peppercorns
4 cups Vegetable Stock (page 97)
1 lemon, juiced

Place soaked, rinsed, and drained lentils in a pot and add 1 quart of fresh water and the bay leaf. Bring to simmer, cover, and cook for 5 minutes or till lentils are soft. Drain, and remove bay leaf.

In a soup pot, heat up olive oil and add onions and sea salt and sauté 10 minutes over medium heat, stirring occasionally. Add the rest of the ingredients, except for the stock and lemon juice, and sauté 5 minutes. Add stock, bring to a boil, then reduce heat, cover, and cook 10 minutes or till lentils are soft. Add lemon juice. Season to taste with salt and pepper.

Variation: Puree one-third to one-half of the soup.

GARBANZO TAHINI SOUP

For the great oud player Sinan Erdemsel.

YIELD: 4 SERVINGS

1/3 cup dried garbanzo beans, soaked overnight, rinsed, and drained
1 bay leaf
1/4 cup tahini
1/4 cup lemon juice
2 tablespoons olive oil
1 onion, chopped
1 leek, chopped
1 1/2 teaspoons sea salt
8 cloves garlic, minced
2 carrots, sliced diagonally
2 teaspoons dried oregano
5 cups Vegetable Stock (page 97)
Freshly cracked black peppercorns
1 teaspoon smoked paprika

Add soaked, rinsed, and drained garbanzos to a pot with 3 cups water and bay leaf, bring to a boil, lower the heat, cover, and simmer for 45 minutes or till garbanzos are tender. Drain garbanzos, removing bay leaf. Set aside.

In a bowl, mix tahini with lemon juice to make a paste, adding cold water as needed. Set aside.

In a hot soup pot, add olive oil, onion, leek, and sea salt and cook 10 minutes over medium-low heat, covered, till onions are slightly caramelized. Add garlic, carrots, and oregano, and cook 5 minutes. Add stock and bring to a simmer. Add black pepper to taste, the smoked paprika, and the tahini-lemon paste and blend well. Stir in the garbanzos. Taste! Add salt or lemon juice if needed.

CREAM OF MUSHROOM SOUP

A few years ago, we were having a bumper crop of chanterelles in the Oakland hills. Ten pounds of beautiful mushrooms were easily found on every hike and for those two months, chanterelle dishes were all over the underground restaurant menus. This soup was a huge hit at a Chris Caswell dinner concert.

YIELD: 4 SERVINGS

1/3 cup raw cashews
4 cups Vegetable Stock (page 97)
3 tablespoons olive oil
1 onion, diced
1 teaspoon sea salt
10 fresh sage leaves
1 sprig fresh thyme
6 cloves garlic, diced
1 stalk celery, diced
1 pound wild mushrooms, cleaned very well and cut into small pieces (Use whatever is in season and available or that you desire. If no wild mushrooms are available, use shiitake, crimini, or portobello.)
1/4 cup dry sherry
Freshly cracked black peppercorns
Fresh parsley, for garnish

In a blender, add cashews and stock and blend till pureed and totally smooth. Set aside.

In a hot frying pan, add olive oil, onions, salt, sage, and thyme and cook over medium-low heat about 10 minutes. Add garlic, celery, and mushrooms and cook 10 minutes, till mushrooms start to break down. Add sherry and cook till alcohol flavor is gone. Pour in the blended cashew-stock mixture. Heat, stirring well, as the cashew cream can stick if left unattended, adding more stock if it is too thick. Season to taste with salt and black pepper. Garnish with fresh parsley.

CREAM OF POTATO SOUP

Thanks to my friends Scott Walton and Sophie Placard for their endless supply of sorrel from their garden. Joëlle Léandre greatly enjoyed this hearty winter soup!

YIELD: 4-6 SERVINGS

1/3 cup raw cashews
4 cups Vegetable Stock (page 97)
3 tablespoons olive oil
1 onion, diced
1 teaspoon sea salt
1 sprig rosemary
10 sage leaves
6 cloves garlic, minced
1 stalk celery, diced
2 pounds fingerling potatoes, peeled, cut into 1/2-inch dice
Large bunch sorrel, chopped
Freshly cracked black peppercorns

In a blender, add cashews and stock. Puree till totally smooth. Set aside.

In a hot frying pan, add olive oil. Add onions, salt, rosemary, and sage and cook over medium-low heat about 10 minutes. Add garlic, celery, and potatoes and cook 5 minutes. Add sorrel and cook till sorrel is broken down and potatoes are cooked, about 10 minutes. Pour in the blended cashew-stock mixture. Bring to a simmer, stirring well as the cashew cream can stick if left unattended, and add more stock if the soup is too thick. Season to taste with salt and pepper.

ROASTED CAULIFLOWER WATERCRESS MISO CHOWDER

YIELD: 4-6 SERVINGS

1/2 pound small creamer potatoes, diced

1 head cauliflower, diced

1/2 teaspoon sea salt

1 tablespoon safflower oil

1 tablespoon olive oil

1 onion, diced

1 leek, diced

5 cloves garlic, minced

1 carrot, minced

1 stalk celery, diced

3 cups Vegetable Stock (page 97)

1/3 cup raw cashews

1/4 cup white miso (saikyo preferable)

1 small bunch watercress

Freshly cracked black peppercorns

Very good quality olive oil, for garnish

In a roasting pan, add potatoes and cauliflower. Sprinkle with 1/2 teaspoon sea salt and the safflower oil. Cover with foil and roast at 425°F for 30 minutes.

Meanwhile, in a frying pan, heat olive oil and add onions and leeks. Over medium-low heat, cook about 10 minutes till slightly caramelized. Add garlic, carrot, and celery and cook 5 minutes over medium heat, stirring occasionally.

Add half of the sautéed vegetables and half of the roasted vegetables to a blender. Add stock, cashews, miso, and watercress to the blender and puree till very smooth. Add the mixture to a pot with the rest of the sautéed and roasted vegetables. Bring to a simmer but do not boil! Season to taste with black pepper. Garnish with a small amount of very good olive oil.

ASPARAGUS MISO CHOWDER

YIELD: 4 SERVINGS

1 onion, diced
2 tablespoons olive oil
5 cloves garlic, minced
1/2 pound small red potatoes or other creamy potatoes, diced
1 pound asparagus, trimmed and cut into 1/2-inch pieces
1/4 cup raw cashews
1/4 cup white miso (saikyo miso is preferable)
2 cups Vegetable Stock (page 97)
Freshly cracked black peppercorns
Smoked paprika, for garnish

In a frying pan, sauté onion in olive oil for about 10 minutes, stirring often, till onion starts to caramelize. Add garlic and potatoes and continue cooking till potatoes are soft. Add asparagus and cook 2 more minutes.

Place half of the cooked vegetables into a blender and add raw cashews, miso, and stock and puree till very smooth. Place the puree into a pot, adding the rest of the cooked vegetables and potatoes.

Season with freshly cracked black peppercorns to taste, and salt if needed. Garnish each bowl with a small amount of smoked paprika.

WHITE GAZPACHO

Credit for this has to go to my shakuhachi student and friend, Manuel Maqueda. Manuel loves food, especially the food of his grandmother's kitchen in Madrid, and loves to share these culinary delights. We often trade music lessons in exchange for him showing me his grandma's ideas. This soup was brand new to me when he showed it to me and I have made it for many events and always with great results!

This version of gazpacho is known as Ajo Blanco, White Garlic Soup, and originates in the Andalusian part of Spain, obviously with Arabic influences. This is insanely simple to make!

YIELD: 4 SERVINGS

3/4 cup raw almonds, peeled (page 45)
2 cloves garlic
1 teaspoon sea salt
1/2 teaspoon white pepper
1/3 cup red wine vinegar
1 small piece of bread (not sourdough!)
3 cups cold water
1/3 cup very high quality extra-virgin olive oil, plus more for drizzling
Ice cubes

Blend all ingredients except the olive oil and ice till very smooth. At the end of the blending, add olive oil and blend till very smooth. Chill soup 2 hours or more. Taste!! Add salt or vinegar if needed. This is a mild-flavored soup.

To serve, divide soup into 4 bowls. Add ice cubes to each bowl. Drizzle a small bit of high quality olive oil into each bowl.

Options: Garnish with seedless green grapes in summer, or pitted cherries in late spring. Diced cucumbers are another good addition.

RED GAZPACHO

There are so many variations on this dish! Some are all pureed, some are chunky, like this one. Some are raw, some cooked, some a combination of raw and cooked. Some are all tomato, some are tomato with peppers, some tomato with cucumber, or tomato with cucumber and peppers. Some add hot or medium-hot peppers to the puree. Follow your instincts and whatever summer bounty is available. This dish is all about the freshness of the summer crop. You cannot hide a low quality tomato in this soup. Explore the variety of heirloom tomatoes to find some amazing variations on this soup!

YIELD: 8 SERVINGS

8 very ripe tomatoes, diced
1 red bell pepper, diced
1 orange bell pepper, diced
1 yellow bell pepper, diced
1/2 red onion, diced
2 cucumbers, peeled, diced
2 cloves garlic
2 teaspoons sea salt
1/3 cup red wine vinegar
1/4 cup cilantro
1/4 cup very high quality extra-virgin olive oil
Ice cubes
1 green onion, chopped, for garnish

Set aside half of the diced tomatoes, peppers, onions, and cucumbers, and add the other half to a blender with the garlic, salt, vinegar, cilantro, and 2 cups cold water. (You may have to do this in 2 batches, depending on the size of your blender.) At the end of the blending, add the olive oil and blend till very smooth.

In a large bowl, combine the blended vegetables with the reserved diced vegetables. Taste! Add salt or vinegar if needed. Add water if it is too thick. If too thin, add a little bit of soup to a blender and add a small piece of bread (not sourdough!) and blend. Then add this back to the soup.

To serve, place ice cubes in each bowl. Add cold soup, and garnish with green onions and drops of olive oil.

For a creamy version, add 1/4 cup raw almonds or raw cashews to the blender with the vegetables.

LEMONGRASS COCONUT SOUP WITH GLASS NOODLES

YIELD: 4 SERVINGS

2 rolls glass noodles (about 2 ounces dried mung bean noodle threads)

2 cups Southeast Asian Stock (page 98)

2 cups coconut milk

2 stalks lemongrass, cut lengthwise, then into 8 pieces, then bruised

1 slice ginger, 1/4 inch thick by 1 inch long

10 makrut lime leaves

1/4 cup soy sauce

1/4 cup palm sugar

1 tablespoon tamarind extract or paste

1-4 Thai chilis, sliced

4 fresh wood ear mushrooms, quartered

1 cup mixed Thai basil, opal basil, and Italian basil, chopped

1/4 pound medium tofu, cut into 1/4-inch cubes

2 tablespoon lime juice

1 green onion, chopped, for garnish

Bring 4 cups of water to a boil. Drop glass noodles in, remove from heat, and stir well. Let sit 3 minutes or till soft. Remove from water and rinse well. Set aside.

In a wok or saucepan, heat up stock and coconut milk with lemongrass, ginger, and lime leaves. Add soy sauce, palm sugar, and tamarind extract. Bring to a simmer. Cook, uncovered, at low heat for 10 minutes or till flavors blend well. Add sliced chilis, wood ears, basil, and tofu. Bring back to a simmer, uncovered, lower heat, and cook 5 minutes. Add lime juice to taste! Add soy sauce or palm sugar, if needed.

To serve, drop glass noodles for one second in hot water to heat them up. Add glass noodles to 4 bowls. Pour soup over noodles. Garnish with green onion and more basil if desired. The lemongrass and ginger slice can be discarded before serving or remind the guests not to chew on it.

Note: Never cover coconut milk while simmering. If you cover anything containing coconut milk while simmering, it will curdle.

JAPANESE-STYLE NOODLE SOUP

YIELD: 2 SERVINGS

2 teaspoons dried wakame

3 cups Kombu Stock (page 98)

1/4 cup mirin

3 tablespoons sake

1/4 cup soy sauce

1/4 pound tofu, cut into 1/2-inch cubes

Oil for deep frying

1/2 recipe of Homemade Noodles (page 84) or Homemade Soba Noodles (page 87)

1 green onion, minced, for garnish

Hydrate the dried wakame in a bowl of water for 10 minutes. Drain, rinse, and set aside.

In a saucepan, heat up stock and add mirin, sake, and soy sauce. Bring to a simmer, cover, lower heat, and cook 3 minutes to blend flavors and evaporate the alcohol.

Deep-fry tofu till golden brown (see page 134).

Cut noodles to desired size. Add noodles to a rapidly boiling pot of water and cook 1 minute or till al dente. Drain and rinse with cold water. Divide noodles into 2 bowls.

Pour hot stock over noodles, garnish with green onion and wakame, and add tofu from the fryer straight into the soup.

CHINESE-STYLE NOODLE SOUP

YIELD: 2 SERVINGS

Soup:
3 cups Kombu Stock (page 97)
1/4 cup soy sauce
3 tablespoons palm sugar
1 tablespoon chinkiang vinegar
1 tablespoon toasted sesame oil

Stir-fry:
1 tablespoon sesame oil (NOT toasted)
2 tablespoons ginger, minced
2 tablespoons garlic, minced
2 red chilis, minced
1 carrot, julienned
3 fresh shiitake mushrooms, slivered
1/2 cup soybean sprouts
6 snow pea pods, julienned
2 fresh wood ear mushrooms, quartered
1/2 teaspoon Sichuan peppercorns, ground in a mortar and pestle
1/2 teaspoon ground white pepper

1/2 recipe Homemade Noodles (page 84), cut to desired size
1 green onion, minced, for garnish
1 tablespoon cilantro, chopped, for garnish

For the soup: In a saucepan, heat up stock with soy sauce, palm sugar, and chinkiang vinegar. Bring to a boil, cover, lower heat, and cook 3 minutes. Add toasted sesame oil.

For the stir-fry: In a hot wok, add sesame oil, ginger, garlic, and chili and stir-fry for 30 seconds. Add carrot, shiitakes, sprouts, snow peas, and wood ears and stir-fry 1 minute, leaving vegetables nice and crisp. Add Sichuan peppercorns and white pepper and combine well.

Drop fresh homemade noodles into a large pot of rapidly boiling water. Cook 1 minute or till al dente. Rinse with cold water. Divide noodles into 2 bowls. Add half the stir-fried vegetables to each bowl. Pour hot stock over the bowls and garnish with green onion and cilantro.

THAI-STYLE NOODLE SOUP

YIELD: 2 SERVINGS

Soup:

3 cups Southeast Asian Stock (page 98)

1/2 cup soy sauce

1/3 cup palm sugar

Juice and zest of 2 limes

Stir-fry:

2 tablespoons coconut oil

1 stalk lemongrass, minced

10 makrut lime leaves, shredded

2 tablespoons garlic, minced

2-10 Thai chilis, minced

1 tablespoon ginger, minced

1/2 red onion, cut into half-moons

1 carrot, julienned

1 cup gai lan (Chinese broccoli), cut into 1-inch lengths

1/2 recipe Homemade Noodles (page 84), cut to desired size

Garnishes:

1/4 cup tofu, cut into 1/2-inch cubes

2 tablespoons basil, chopped

2 tablespoons Thai basil, chopped

2 tablespoons cilantro, chopped

1 green onion, minced

For the soup: In a saucepan, heat up stock with soy sauce and palm sugar. Bring to a boil, cover, lower heat, and cook 1 minute. Remove from heat and add lime juice and zest.

For the stir-fry: In a hot wok, add coconut oil, lemongrass, makrut leaves, garlic, chilis, and ginger and stir-fry 30 seconds. Add red onion, carrots, and gai lan and stir-fry 3 minutes.

Drop fresh noodles in a large pot of rapidly boiling water. Cook 1 minute or till al dente. Rinse with cold water.

Divide noodles into 2 bowls. Add half the stir-fried vegetables to each bowl. Pour hot stock over the bowls, add tofu, and garnish with basil, cilantro, and green onions.

VEGETABLES

LATKES (POTATO PANCAKES)

This is the first dish I learned how to make! My grandmother, my Aunt Rose, and my mother made these for Chanukah and other Jewish holidays. And I took over the latke duty early on as a child. These are simple to make and who does not love a fried potato?!? No one in my family ever measured anything when making these but here is an approximate recipe to get started with.

YIELD: 4 SERVINGS

3 large russet potatoes (not peeled)
1 onion
3 tablespoons yama-imo, grated
Salt and pepper
1/3 cup matzoh meal, or as needed
Oil for frying

Grate potatoes into a bowl. Press out and discard the liquid from the grated potatoes. Grate the onion into the potato. Grate yama-imo and add to the mix along with salt and pepper to taste. Add the matzoh meal. Do not over-mix or the pancakes will be rubbery.

Heat about 1/2 inch of oil in a frying pan.

Add 1/4 cup of pancake mixture to the hot oil, being careful not to overcrowd the pan! Fry on one side till the edges start to brown. Do NOT turn prematurely. As is the rule of all pancakes, never turn more than one time. No exceptions if you want the ultimate texture and the least fat absorption. Turn over and fry on the other side till crisp.

Serve hot with Applesauce (page 52).

Variations: Latkes are traditionally made with 100% potatoes. You can vary this by adding other root vegetables such as celery root, sweet potatoes (satsuma imo, in particular, work very well in this recipe!), and, for a colorful latke, beets!

Variation: Latkes, Tokyo Style.

One cold winter evening in Tokyo, I was invited, along with my partner at the time, to some friends' home (Shing and Yoko) for dinner. It was my last evening in Japan for this particular visit. They asked me to prepare something from my culture that night and I decided to make latkes, the first dish I learned to make. While I was frying the latkes, I noticed my friend Shing grating daikon and putting out small dishes of soy sauce for the four of us. As I started to place latkes, fresh out of the oil, onto the table, I noticed my three Japanese friends reaching for the grated daikon, putting it on the latkes, and then taking a piece of latke with daikon and dipping it in soy sauce and eating it. "What are you doing?" I exclaimed. "The bowl of homemade applesauce is intended to go with the latkes." Shing then declared, "We always serve fried foods with grated daikon and soy sauce." Of course! Daikon helps break down fat and thus is always served with fried foods in Japanese culture! Thus a Japanese-Jewish fusion was created and since that night I have always served latkes both with applesauce and with grated daikon and shoyu, giving diners two options.

For this variation, prepare latkes as in the recipe above. Top latkes with grated daikon and give each person a small dish of soy sauce for dipping.

Options: Freshly grated wasabi can be a wonderful addition!

ROASTED CORN SALAD

YIELD: SERVES 4-6

One of my signature summer dishes. We serve this on its own or sometimes stuffed into small round zucchini or eggplants.

4 ears corn, kernels cut from cob
1 red pepper, diced
1 jalapeño, seeded and minced
2 cloves garlic, minced
2 tablespoons grapeseed oil
1 teaspoon sea salt
Zest and juice of 2 limes
3 green onions, chopped
2 tablespoons cilantro, chopped
10 sage leaves, chopped

Combine corn kernels, pepper, jalapeño, garlic, grapeseed oil, and salt in a roasting pan and cover tightly. Roast at 425°F for 35 minutes. The corn should start to lightly caramelize. Place in a bowl and add the rest of the ingredients and toss gently. Serve hot or cold.

For a nice plating idea, we have often served this salad in small, round, partly hollowed-out zucchini that were first roasted or steamed for beautiful, edible bowls.

ROASTED/MASHED ROOT VEGETABLES

My take on the classic mashed potato dish.

YIELD: 4-6 SERVINGS

1/3 cup raw cashews
1 celery root, peeled and diced
1 satsuma imo, peeled and diced
Several creamer potatoes, peeled and diced
1 turnip, peeled and diced
1 parsnip, peeled and diced
1 teaspoon sea salt
2 tablespoons grapeseed oil
3 tablespoons extra-virgin olive oil
1/2 teaspoon black pepper
Optional: 1/4 cup chopped fresh dill, parsley, or basil

In a blender make cashew cream by blending the cashews with 1 cup water till smooth. Set aside.

Peel and dice all the root vegetables, put them in a roasting pan, and toss with the salt and grapeseed oil. Cover tightly and roast at 425°F for 40 minutes.

Mash the roasted root vegetables with a potato masher. Add the cashew cream to this mixture along with the olive oil and black pepper and blend well. For variation, add chopped fresh dill, basil, or parsley.

SAUTÉED RAPINI WITH GARLIC AND OLIVES

YIELD: 2-4 SERVINGS

2 tablespoons olive oil
10 cloves garlic, minced
1 bunch rapini, chopped
10 green olives, pitted and chopped
1/3 cup red wine
Black pepper

In a hot frying pan, add oil and garlic and sauté
one minute. Add rapini and olives and sauté for 5
minutes. Add wine and cook 1 minute. Add black pepper
to taste and salt if needed. Serve with pasta!

STIR-FRIED ONG CHOY WITH GARLIC AND FERMENTED BEAN CURD

Ong choy, also known as water spinach or morning glory stems, is a very inexpensive, flavorful, and nutritious vegetable that grows in fresh water.

YIELD: 2-4 SERVINGS

1 large bunch ong choy, thoroughly cleaned and cut into 1-inch pieces
1 tablespoon peanut oil
10 cloves garlic, minced
1 teaspoon sea salt
1 teaspoon fermented bean curd
1 tablespoon shaoshing
2 tablespoons Kombu Stock (page 97)

Blanch the ong choy by dropping it into a large pot of boiling water for 10 seconds. Immediately drain and rinse in cold water to stop cooking.

In a hot wok, add oil and garlic, stir-frying for 30 seconds. Add ong choy, salt, and fermented bean curd and stir-fry 2 minutes. Add shaoshing and stock and cook another 30 seconds. Adjust for salt, if needed.

STIR-FRIED COLLARDS

While in college in the South, I encountered collard greens. The Southern approach to cooking greens was to cook them down for hours so they had no flavor or texture, and then build up a flavor profile with some fatty pig parts. No thanks to that absurd way of destroying vegetables! However, I quickly discovered these greens are so flavorful on their own with a great deal of texture if cooked well. Blanching them and using them whole to wrap other ingredients in is a huge favorite. Stir-frying them as in this recipe is one of the numerous great ways to enjoy this amazing and highly nutritious vegetable.

YIELD: SERVES 2

1 tablespoon olive oil

5 cloves garlic, minced

10 large collards, julienned

2 teaspoons sake

1 tablespoon mirin

1 tablespoon soy sauce

In a hot wok, add olive oil and garlic and stir-fry for 30 seconds. Add greens and stir-fry 2 minutes. Add the rest of the ingredients and stir-fry 30 seconds.

Serve with hot rice.

STIR-FRIED GAI LAN WITH GARLIC AND GINGER

YIELD: SERVES 2-4

1 bunch gai lan (Chinese broccoli)
1 quart boiling water with 1/8 teaspoon baking soda added
1 tablespoon non-toasted sesame oil
1 teaspoon fermented Chinese black beans
10 cloves garlic
1 tablespoon ginger, minced
2 teaspoons palm sugar
2 tablespoons Kombu Stock (page 97)
1 tablespoon shaoshing
1 tablespoon soy sauce

Blanch gai lan in the boiling water with the baking soda, for 30 seconds. Remove greens from the water, drain them, and place on a plate.

In a hot wok, add the oil, black beans, garlic, and ginger and stir-fry for 30 seconds. Add palm sugar, stock, shaoshing, and soy sauce and cook 1 minute. Pour sauce over the gai lan. Serve with rice and a tofu or tempeh dish.

COLLARD ROLLS STUFFED WITH PEACH-ROASTED TEMPEH, WILD RICE PILAF, AND PUMPKIN PUREE

Growing up in Brooklyn with Jewish Eastern-European grandparents, I was very fond of stuffed cabbage rolls! My mom and my Aunt Rose and other relatives would make stewed meatballs with raisins, wrapped in cabbage leaves, in tomato sauce. My fondness for wrapping flavorful ingredients in leaves and stewing or roasting them in sauces has constantly evolved over the years, and collards are my leaf of choice. Of course you can substitute cabbage leaves, particularly savoy cabbage for its wonderful texture and flavor. This is one of those dishes where improvisation is constantly employed, as it is never made the same way twice. Sometimes tempeh is used, marinated, roasted, smoked, or fried in various ways and sometimes a lentil or bean ball is employed. Sometimes a grain is in there, sometimes a variety of roasted mashed root vegetables. Sometimes pumpkin, sometimes sweet potato. There are no limits to coming up with amazing versions of this idea!

YIELD: SERVES 4

8 large collard leaves
1 recipe Pumpkin Puree (butternut squash works very well for this recipe!) (page 30)
1 recipe Wild Rice Pilaf (page 83)
1 recipe Peach-Roasted Tempeh (page 148)

Steam the collard leaves for 2 minutes, till pliable. With the back of a knife or your thumb, press down on the spine of each leaf till you rupture the spine, crushing it yet not tearing it.

Place the collard leaves on a board. Place 2 tablespoons pumpkin puree on each leaf. Place 2 tablespoons wild rice pilaf on top of the pumpkin puree. Add some slices of peach-roasted tempeh on top of the pilaf. Roll up and fold tightly. Steam the rolls for 10 minutes. (You can roll these in advance and then steam them to reheat.)

Variations: Use other fruit-roasted tempeh.

Use roasted mashed root vegetables instead of pumpkin puree.

Use other grains instead of wild rice pilaf.

EGGPLANT ROLLATINI

YIELD: 4-6 SERVINGS

1 large eggplant cut lengthwise into 1/2-inch slices
Sea salt
Olive oil
Basil leaves
1 recipe Almond Ricotta (page 45)
1 recipe Basic Tomato Sauce (page 38)

Lightly salt the eggplant and brush it with oil. Place eggplant slices on a baking sheet and roast at 400°F for 10 minutes. The eggplant will become soft and rollable but is not fully cooked.

Place 2 or 3 basil leaves on each eggplant slice. Add 2 tablespoons almond ricotta and roll up tightly. Place eggplant rolls in a baking dish. Cover with the tomato sauce, cover the dish, and bake at 350°F for 30 minutes or till piping hot. Serve with pasta and a green vegetable.

YUZU CURRY PASTE

A unique sour curry paste pairing the delightful flavors of Thai curries with the wonderful Japanese citrus, yuzu.

YIELD: ABOUT 1 CUP

2 teaspoons cumin seeds

1 tablespoon coriander seeds

1 teaspoon black peppercorns

1 yuzu, halved and seeded

2 stalks lemongrass

4 cloves garlic

10 Thai chilis

1 tablespoon fresh minced ginger

1 tablespoon fermented Chinese bean curd

10 yuzu leaves

3 tablespoons New Mexico chili powder or other sweet red pepper powder

1 teaspoon sea salt

Toast the cumin, coriander, and peppercorns for a few minutes in a hot frying pan over low heat, stirring often. You can make this paste quickly by putting all ingredients in a food processor or you can take more time and pound it out in a mortar and pestle. If using a mortar and pestle, cut all your ingredients into small pieces. Add one ingredient at a time and grind it down to a paste. Then add another ingredient till all the flavors are combined and a very aromatic and spicy paste is developed.

This paste lasts, covered tightly in the fridge, for up to 2 weeks!

TEMPEH, TOFU & BEANS

HOMEMADE TEMPEH

If you have only had packaged industrialized tempeh, trying this may change your life!

YIELD: 1 3/4 POUNDS TEMPEH

1 pound dry, organic, non-GMO soybeans
1 teaspoon rice vinegar
Tempeh starter/spores (amount will depend on the producer of the spores, please read the
   instructions that come with your spores)

You will need the following equipment:
Bowl for mixing
Rolling pin
Perforated bags, or trays, or organic bamboo leaves or organic banana leaves if possible
Pot to cook beans
Strainer
Clean kitchen towels
A way to keep the tempeh at 80-88 degrees (I use a low-temperature oven (dehydrator).
One can rig up an incubator using several different methods; I suggest going online to look up
various methods if you do not have a dehydrator.)

Key things to consider: Sanitation: With all fermentation, we are looking to grow a controlled microorganism in an environment that contains something for this microorganism to eat and thus grow. We are looking to ensure that no other microorganism develops alongside. Sanitize your hands, spoons, bowls, and mixing implements before making tempeh.

Quality of ingredients: Use the finest organic, non-GMO beans. You will taste the difference. Your body and the environment will feel the difference.

Steps in making tempeh: Crack dry beans (if using a machine, crack the beans first, otherwise soak the beans first to crack by hands later). Soak beans 8-14 hours, then rinse and drain.

Cook the beans. Organic soybeans that are not too old usually take 45 minutes to cook. Quality and age of beans may cause them to take longer.

If not using a machine, crack beans by hand, after soaking (or after cooking).

Place cooked beans in a large bowl. Add cold water to cover the beans. With clean hands, rub the beans between your palms. The beans will break open, causing the hulls to come off. This is a very important step that cannot be skipped. The hulls must be removed! The hulls will rise to the surface of the water. Skim the hulls and discard them. It is essential to remove at least 90 percent of the hulls or the tempeh will not ferment well. Repeat rubbing the beans and removing the hulls till you have removed 90 percent of the hulls and the beans are broken up.

Drain beans. Dry beans very well (moisture is the enemy of tempeh spores). First drain them in a strainer or colander and then place the beans in a single layer on towels. Let them dry for an hour. Again, this step cannot be skipped!

Add the vinegar and mix well. Add tempeh starter and mix well. (Starter amounts vary! Use the instructions that come with the starter you purchase.)

You are now ready to "package" the tempeh. Bags or leaves must be perforated in order for the spores to breath. Too much humidity in the bags will cause spoilage and other molds to develop. Using a sterilized pin, make holes every 3/4 inch in the bags.

For pint-size bags, I use 1/2 pound of cooked and inoculated beans. For gallon bags I use 1 3/4 pounds. Do not overstuff! The tempeh spores can only grow in layers of 1-inch thickness.

Incubate the bags of tempeh at 80-88°F for 24-48 hours. Around the 12th hour you will notice things are developing. Turn off your heat source in the 16th hour. At that point, the tempeh is generating its own heat. Too high a temperature kills the spores we are trying to develop. Too high a heat also allows other bacteria to grow, which is, of course, undesirable.

Around 24-36 hours you will see a full cake of tempeh developed. Some black or grey spots are natural, as is the snowy white "frost" covering your tempeh. This is the real stuff, not pasteurized, frozen, and shipped from afar and sitting on a shelf. It is a very different type of food as it is still alive. Ideally, use the tempeh immediately. Go straight from incubator to fryer or to marinade as soon as the tempeh finishes developing. Otherwise, freeze the tempeh once it is finished developing. If you keep it at room temperature or at 80-88°F, it will continue to develop. Overripe tempeh is not ruined but will have a very strong taste and very dark color.

Always cook fresh tempeh thoroughly!!! I must stress this. Tempeh is a mycelium. All wild and cultivated mushrooms should be cooked thoroughly to be totally digestible. Steam, sauté, fry, stir-fry, use your imagination. You have just made one of the least expensive and nutritious sources of protein known to our planet.

And now for some ideas of how to use this wonderful ingredient.

The most basic, simple, and delightful thing is to simply cut tempeh into strips or cubes or triangles and fry them up and serve them with a sauce. It is a fast and easy way to prepare tempeh and the variety of dipping sauces is limitless.

Simply preheat oil. Use a high-temperature oil such as grapeseed or coconut. Fry tempeh on each side till golden brown and serve asap.

Note: To find tempeh cultures, go online and do a search for "tempeh starter" or "tempeh spores." There are limited options where to purchase these in the United States and in other countries.

And support your local tempeh maker if you have one. I fully support and endorse my friends in Oakland at Rhizocali Tempeh, a small business owned and operated by two wonderful women just a few blocks from my home and kitchen.

HOMEMADE TOFU

Nothing beats the texture and flavor of freshly made, still-warm tofu!

YIELD: ABOUT 1 POUND

1 gallon homemade soy milk
1 teaspoon nigari

You will also need:
A tofu mold
Cheesecloth

Bring 1 gallon of soy milk to a boil. Lower heat and let simmer, covered, for 15 minutes. Remove from heat.

Mix nigari with 1 cup cold water. Slowly add the nigari mixture to the soy milk and gently stir, cover, and let sit for 40 minutes. As the mixture cools, curds will form.

Pour curds into a mold that is lined with cheesecloth and then press with a weight on top. The texture and firmness of the finished tofu depends on how much water you press from it. Leave the tofu to drain until it is the desired texture. The longer you press, the firmer the resulting tofu.

Note: Best to use homemade soy milk!! If using packaged, you must use unflavored with no additives; the only ingredients can be soy beans and water (no sweeteners, no thickeners, no salt, etc.).

TOFU CUTLETS

A simple, delightful everyday dish.

YIELD: 2-4 SERVINGS

1 pound firm tofu, cut into 1/2-inch cutlets (8 pieces)

Arrange 3 bowls in a row, containing the following ingredients:

Bowl 1: 1/2 cup flour mixed with 1/4 teaspoon salt.

Bowl 2: 1/2 cup soy milk mixed with 1/4 teaspoon salt.

Bowl 3: 1/2 cup cornmeal mixed with 1/4 teaspoon salt, 1/2 teaspoon oregano, 1/2 teaspoon black pepper, 1/2 teaspoon minced rosemary, 1/2 teaspoon thyme, and 2 tablespoons nutritional yeast.

Dip tofu pieces in the flour, turn, and dip on other side. Dip the same tofu now in the soy milk mixture, coating both sides, and then dip in the cornmeal mixture, coating both sides. Repeat these steps for all tofu pieces.

On a baking tray lightly coated with oil, bake the cutlets at 425°F for 30 minutes or till crisp. Alternatively, deep-fry till golden brown. They can also be pan-fried.

Options: This recipe works just as well with tempeh or seitan.

TEA-SMOKED TOFU

Smoking takes tofu to a whole new level of delightfulness! Infinite varieties of marinades and smoking woods can keep your tastebuds endlessly amused and engaged. Smoked tofu is fine by itself (especially if served with a nice Asian-style mustard!). Or you can dice it and add to noodle soups or salads, or slice it on sandwiches.

YIELD: 2-4 SERVINGS, OR CAN BE USED AS A GARNISH FOR SOUPS OR SALADS.

1 pound firm tofu

Marinade:
2 tablespoons soy sauce
1 tablespoon shaoshing
2 tablespoons Kombu Stock (page 97)
A few Sichuan peppercorns
2 teaspoons palm sugar
1/8-inch slice ginger, about 1 inch long

1 tablespoon oolong tea leaves

Cut tofu into slabs 2/3 inch thick. Place pieces on a clean kitchen towel. Place another towel on top of the tofu. Place a board on top and then place a cast iron pan or other heavy object on the board. Press the tofu for 15 minutes.

Mix all marinade ingredients in a bowl. Marinate the pressed tofu for 1-2 hours, turning a couple of times. Soak the oolong tea leaves in water during this time.

Prepare your smoker. Remove tea leaves from water and drop them on your coals or smoking pan. Smoke tofu over tea for 15 minutes or till it starts to brown. Be careful not to over-smoke or it gets overwhelming. A combination of cherry wood and oolong tea leaves makes a wonderful smoke for tofu!

FLAT TOFU NOODLES WITH SESAME OIL

This dish came about from my friendship with Kevin Stong, owner of Tofu Yu in Berkeley. Tofu Yu is a small artisan tofu shop, making very high quality tofu in small batches out of a tiny space. One of their unique creations is flat tofu, a rare style of tofu that originates in Harbin, China. The machine used produces a tofu that comes out in dry sheets, with a wonderful texture!

YIELD: 2-4 SERVINGS

1/2 pound flat tofu, cut into noodles
2 green onions, chopped
2 tablespoons toasted sesame oil
3 tablespoons cilantro, chopped
2 tablespoons soy sauce
1 teaspoon palm sugar

Cut the flat tofu sheets into noodles. Drop the noodles into a pot of boiling water for 1 minute, then drain. Place noodles in a bowl, add the rest of the ingredients, and toss to mix.

ORANGE TOFU

Another favorite Chinese dish that finds itself on many winter menus when oranges are ripe.

YIELD: 4 SERVINGS

1 pound firm tofu, drained and pressed, cut into triangles
Oil for deep-frying
1 tablespoon sesame oil (not toasted)
10 cloves garlic, minced
20 dried tien tsen chilis
1 teaspoon Sichuan peppercorns, pounded in a mortar and pestle
1/8 teaspoon star anise
2 cups orange juice, freshly squeezed
1 tablespoon shaoshing
2 tablespoons soy sauce
1 teaspoon dark soy sauce
2 teaspoons cornstarch dissolved in 1 tablespoon water
1 pound broccoli or choy sum, cut into florets
Cilantro, for garnish

Deep-fry tofu till crisp, then set aside.

In a hot wok, add sesame oil. Stir-fry garlic and chilis for 30 seconds. Add Sichuan peppercorns and star anise and stir fry a few seconds. Add orange juice. Over medium heat, cook till it reduces in volume by half. Add shaoshing, soy sauce, and dark soy sauce. Add cornstarch mixture and stir-fry till it thickens. Add fried tofu and coat well.

Blanch the broccoli or choy sum for 10 seconds in a pot of boiling water.

For plating: Place broccoli or choy sum in a circle and fill the circle with the orange-sauced tofu.

TOFU WITH BLACK BEAN SAUCE

Ever since I was a child I have loved black bean sauce! This is one of my everyday, simple dishes to make at home, and it shows up on various menus.

YIELD: 4 SERVINGS

Sauce:
1 tablespoon shaoshing
2 tablespoons palm sugar
2 tablespoons soy sauce
2 teaspoons dark soy sauce
3/4 cup Kombu Stock (page 97)

Slurry:
2 teaspoons cornstarch dissolved in 2 tablespoons water

1 pound tofu, cut into small triangles
Oil for deep-frying
2 tablespoons peanut oil
3 tablespoons garlic, minced
4 dried tien tsen chilis, minced
1 tablespoon fermented black beans, rinsed and minced
1 onion, cut into half moons
1 carrot, cut thin diagonally
1 zucchini, cut into half moons

Mix sauce ingredients in a bowl and set aside. Mix slurry ingredients and set aside.

The tofu can be deep-fried till crisp or added to the dish at the end and simply heated up. (The texture is far superior if fried and absorbs the sauce better.)

In a hot wok, add the peanut oil, garlic, chilis and fermented black beans and stir-fry for 30 seconds. Add onion, carrot, and zucchini and stir-fry 2 minutes. Add sauce ingredients and cook till it starts to bubble. Add tofu and cook another 30 seconds. Add slurry and cook till the sauce thickens, and a few seconds more to remove the starch flavor.

Serve over hot rice along with some stir-fried greens.

FRIED TEMPEH

The best way to eat freshly made tempeh is to fry it up!

1/8-1/4 pound tempeh per person
Oil for deep-frying

Heat oil to a temperture of 350° F to 385° F for deep-frying. Cut tempeh into cubes or slices and deep-fry till golden brown. Serve immediately with a sauce or simply salt. Or use in your favorite tempeh recipe.

TEMPEH SCRAMBLE (ITALIAN)

A favorite breakfast food.

YIELD: 2-4 SERVINGS

1/2 pound tempeh
2 tablespoons olive oil
1/2 yellow onion, diced
1 teaspoon sea salt
1/2 red bell pepper, diced
1 carrot, diced
1 cup diced broccoli
2 cloves garlic, minced
1 teaspoon oregano
1/2 teaspoon thyme
1/2 teaspoon rosemary
1/2 teaspoon turmeric
2 tablespoons dry white wine
1 tablespoon lemon juice
2 tablespoons basil, chopped

Steam tempeh for 20 minutes, then crumble it up and set aside.

In a frying pan, heat olive oil and add onion and salt and sauté for 5 minutes. Add the rest of the vegetables and spices and sauté another 5 minutes. Add tempeh and cook 2 more minutes. Add wine and cook 30 seconds. Add lemon juice and basil and combine well.

TEMPEH SCRAMBLE (MEXICAN)

YIELD: 2-4 SERVINGS

1/2 pound tempeh
2 tablespoons olive oil
1/2 yellow onion, diced
1 teaspoon sea salt
1/2 red bell pepper, diced
1 carrot, diced
1 serrano chili, seeded, diced
2 cloves garlic, minced
1 stalk celery, diced
1/2 teaspoon turmeric
1 teaspoon ground cumin
1 teaspoon oregano
1 teaspoon ancho chili powder
2 tablespoons lime juice
2 tablespoons cilantro, chopped

Steam tempeh for 20 minutes, then crumble it up and set aside.

In a frying pan, heat olive oil and add onion and salt and sauté for 5 minutes. Add the rest of the vegetables and spices and sauté another 5 minutes. Add tempeh and cook 2 more minutes. Add lime juice and cilantro and combine well.

TEMPEH SCRAMBLE (INDIAN)

YIELD: 2-4 SERVINGS

1/2 pound tempeh
2 tablespoons olive oil
1 tomato, chopped
1/2 yellow onion, diced
2 cloves garlic, minced
1 jalapeño, seeded, diced
1/2 teaspoon ginger, minced
1/2 teaspoon turmeric
1/2 teaspoon ground cumin
3/4 teaspoon ground coriander
1/2 red bell pepper, diced
1 carrot, diced
2 tablespoons lime juice
1 teaspoon salt
2 tablespoons cilantro, chopped

Steam tempeh for 20 minutes, then crumble it up and set aside.

In a frying pan, heat olive oil and add tomato, onion, garlic, jalapeño, ginger, turmeric, cumin, and coriander and sauté for 5 minutes. Add red pepper and carrot and sauté another 5 minutes. Add tempeh and cook 2 more minutes. Add lime juice, salt, and cilantro and serve hot.

SMOKED TEMPEH

My second favorite way to eat tempeh is to smoke it! Of course, you can smoke it and then fry it for over-the-top tempeh goodness! Different types of wood will produce a very different taste and aroma. I prefer cherry or alder or apple wood, in particular. Mesquite and hickory can give very strong, somewhat meaty, aromas and tastes to tempeh.

Before you smoke tempeh you will want to marinate it or at least rub it with oil. Use an oil with a very high smoking point, such as safflower, peanut, or rice bran.

Soak wood chips a half hour or more before smoking! Stovetop smokers are available and it is relatively easy to rig up your own stovetop smoker using a wok and chopsticks.

The old-fashioned way of smoking is to heat up your barbecue and get coals going. Drain wood chips and put the chips on the heated coals to begin smoking. Place tempeh on grill, cover, and smoke 10-15 minutes till you get nice grill marks. Turn over and smoke 2-3 more minutes.

TEMPEH WITH PEACH BARBECUE SAUCE

One of countless peach dishes and sauces I have come up with, inspired by the Masumoto family farm and their incredible peaches!

YIELD: 4-8 SERVINGS

1 pound tempeh
Olive oil for brushing tempeh
Peach or apple wood for smoking
Oil for deep-frying
3 cups Peach Barbecue Sauce (page 48)

Brush the tempeh slab with olive oil and smoke it over apple or peach wood for 20 minutes. Let cool and cut into triangles. Deep-fry the smoked tempeh till golden brown and crisp. Simmer lightly in the barbecue sauce before serving.

TEMPEH BACON

I often question why vegans and vegetarians, myself included, often name things after products and industries we find ethically problematic. Whatever we call these various nut-based "cheeses" and soy, gluten, and other protein alternatives, they provide wonderful mouthfeel as well as exceptional flavors.

YIELD: ABOUT 6 SERVINGS

Marinade:
2 tablespoons maple syrup
1 tablespoon umeboshi vinegar
1 tablespoon cider vinegar
2 tablespoons soy sauce
3 tablespoons grapeseed oil

1/2 pound tempeh

Combine the marinade ingredients and marinate tempeh at least 2 hours. Smoke over apple wood for 20 minutes, basting the tempeh regularly. Cut in very thin strips.

One can smoke the tempeh first, then drop it in the marinade, then slice it and pan fry it (adding the marinade to the pan) for a variation.

TEMPEH CHAR SIU

I often serve this as part of an appetizer plate. This is also wonderful as a filling for wontons or steamed dumplings!

YIELD: 4-6 SERVINGS

1 pound tempeh, cut into 1/2-inch cubes

Char Siu sauce:
5 cloves garlic
1 tablespoon minced ginger
3 tablespoons red fermented bean curd
2 tablespoons soy sauce
3 tablespoons shaoshing
2 tablespoons palm sugar
1 teaspoon 5-spice powder
2 tablespoons Kombu Stock (page 97)
2 tablespoons toasted sesame oil

2 tablespoons sesame oil (non-toasted)

Steam the tempeh for 20 minutes.

Heat a broiler.

In a blender, puree the sauce ingredients and set aside.

In a hot wok, add sesame oil. Add tempeh and half the sauce and stir-fry for 10 minutes, till the tempeh starts to brown. Add the rest of the sauce and remove from heat. Place tempeh in its sauce on a baking sheet in one layer. Broil till it browns and slightly chars.

TEMPEH TERIYAKI

A simple Japanese dish with a lot of flavor and texture!

YIELD: 2 SERVINGS

1/2 pound tempeh cut into 1/3-inch strips and deep-fried (page 134)
2 tablespoons sesame oil (not toasted!)
1 onion, sliced thin
4 cloves garlic, minced
2 teaspoons ginger, minced
20 snow peas, deveined
2 tablespoons soy sauce
2 tablespoons sake
2 tablespoons mirin
1/3 cup of any stock (pages 97-98)
1/2 teaspoon cornstarch mixed with 1 tablespoon water
Basil, for garnish

Set aside the deep-fried tempeh.

In a hot wok, heat up sesame oil and add onions, garlic, ginger, and snow peas. Stir-fry over high heat for 2 minutes. Add soy sauce, sake, mirin, and stock and stir-fry 10 seconds or till very bubbly. Add the cornstarch slurry and stir-fry 10 seconds. Add tempeh and garnish with basil.

TEMPEH LARB

This is one of my personal favorite ways to serve tempeh. This is my vegetarian version of a well known Thai/Laotian dish and I have served it at numerous underground restaurant events and catering jobs.

YIELD: 4-6 SERVINGS

2 tablespoons brown rice
3 tablespoons soy sauce
3 tablespoons palm sugar
1/4 cup lime juice
1/2 pound tempeh, cut in 1/4-inch cubes
Oil for deep-frying
2 tablespoons coconut oil
1 stalk lemongrass, minced
4 cloves garlic, minced
3 teaspoons ginger, minced
1-10 Thai chilis, minced
1/2 cup peas
1/2 red onion, diced
1/4 cup Thai basil, chopped
1/4 cup mint, chopped
1/4 cup basil, chopped
1/4 cup cilantro, chopped
Lettuce leaves for wrapping

In a hot frying pan, over medium-low heat, toast the rice. Shake the pan continuously for 2 minutes till the rice is giving off a nutty aroma. Put rice in a mortar and pestle and crush it till it is powdery. Set aside.

Combine soy sauce, palm sugar, and lime juice and set aside.

Deep-fry tempeh till golden brown and crisp. Set aside.

In a hot wok, add the coconut oil. Add lemongrass, garlic, ginger, and chilis and stir-fry 30 seconds. Add peas and onion and stir-fry another minute. Add basil, mint, cilantro, and Thai basil and stir-fry 10 seconds.

Add the soy sauce mixture and stir-fry another minute. Add the toasted rice powder and fried tempeh and stir together. Serve with lettuce leaves and wrap parcels of the larb in lettuce.

TAMARIND TEMPEH

Another wonderful, fragrant, delightful dish from Southeast Asia.

YIELD: 2-4 SERVINGS

1 tablespoon cornstarch
1/2 pound tempeh, cut into 1/2-inch cubes
Oil for deep-frying
3 tablespoons soy sauce
2 tablespoons tamarind extract
4 tablespoons palm sugar
3/4 cup any stock (pages 97-98)
2 tablespoons coconut oil
2 teaspoons minced ginger
1 clove garlic, minced
1-10 Thai chilis, minced
1 red onion, cut in half moons
1 cup peas
1 carrot, julienned
3 tablespoons cilantro, for garnish

Dissolve cornstarch by whisking into 2 tablespoons water and set aside.

Deep-fry tempeh till golden brown and crisp, and set aside.

In a bowl, combine soy sauce, tamarind extract, palm sugar, and stock, then set aside.

In a hot wok, add coconut oil. Add ginger, garlic, and chilis and stir-fry for 30 seconds. Add onions, peas, and carrots and stir-fry another 3 minutes. Add the soy sauce/tamarind mixture and stir-fry till it begins to bubble. Add cornstarch mixture and stir-fry another 30 seconds. Garnish with cilantro and serve with hot rice.

TEMPEH DENGAKU

I dared to serve this at a dinner concert with Japanese musicians (Kaoru Kakizakai and Yodo Kurahashi II). A very traditional Japanese sauce but on an ingredient mostly unknown till recently in Japan. Yuzu, when available, is to be used in this sauce!! Fresh yuzu is divine but the bottled juice is suitable when not in season.

YIELD: 2-4 SERVINGS

1/2 pound tempeh
Oil for deep-frying

Dengaku Sauce:
2 tablespoons white miso
2 tablespoons tahini
2 tablespoons mirin
1 tablespoon maple syrup
1 tablespoon Kombu Stock (page 97)
1 teaspoon toasted sesame oil
2 teaspoons yuzu juice (lemon or lime can be a substitute)
1 tablespoon green onion, minced, for garnish
A few kaiware (daikon sprouts), for garnish
Shiso leaf, for garnish

For a crisp dengaku, deep-fry tempeh till golden brown. Or you can steam the tempeh for 20 minutes. Or roast it, uncovered, for 20 minutes at 425°F.

Combine all sauce ingredients in a bowl. Top the cooked (steamed or fried or roasted) tempeh with the sauce. Place under broiler till it starts to bubble and lightly brown, about 5 minutes. Garnish with green onion, kaiware, and shiso leaf.

LEMONGRASS TEMPEH

Thai/Viet flavors for the win!

YIELD: 2-4 SERVINGS

1 teaspoon cornstarch

3 tablespoons soy sauce

1 teaspoon dark soy sauce

1/2 cup any stock (page 97-98)

3 tablespoons palm sugar

1/2 pound tempeh, cut into small triangles

Oil for deep-frying

2 tablespoons coconut oil

1 stalk lemongrass, minced

3 cloves garlic, minced

1 teaspoon ginger, minced

2-8 red and green Thai chilis, minced

1 onion, cut in half moons

1 small zucchini, cut in 1/4-inch rounds

2 tablespoons basil or Thai basil or a combination, for garnish

Dissolve cornstarch in 1 tablespoon water, whisk, and set aside.

Combine soy sauce, dark soy sauce, stock, and palm sugar in a bowl. Set aside.

Deep-fry tempeh till golden brown and crisp; set aside.

In a hot wok, add coconut oil and immediately add lemongrass, garlic, ginger, and chilis and stir-fry 30 seconds. Add onion and zucchini and stir-fry another minute. Add the soy sauce/palm sugar combination and stir-fry till the liquid starts to boil. Whisk again the cornstarch slurry and add it to the wok. Stir-fry 30 seconds till it thickens slightly.

Garnish with basil and serve.

TEMPEH WITH SOUR YUZU CURRY SERVED IN YUZU BOWLS

A Japanese/Thai fusion improvisation that was written down for posterity.

YIELD: 2-4 SERVINGS

1/2 pound tempeh, cut into 3/4-inch cubes
Oil for deep-frying
1/2 tablespoon coconut oil
1/3 cup yuzu curry paste (page 124)
1/4 cup palm sugar
1/4 cup soy sauce
3 cups coconut milk
1 cup kabocha, cut in small slices
10 Thai eggplants, halved
1 cup basil leaves
10 long beans, cut into 1-inch pieces

For the bowls:

1 yuzu bowl per person (see page 30)

Steam tempeh for 20 minutes or deep-fry till crisp.

In a hot wok, add coconut oil. Add curry paste and stir-fry 2 minutes or till very fragrant.

Add palm sugar, soy sauce, and coconut milk, whisk together, bring to a boil, lower heat, and cook for 10 minutes. Do NOT cover. If you cover coconut milk while simmering, it will curdle.

Add kabocha, eggplant, basil, and long beans. Cook 10 minutes or till vegetables are done. Add tempeh, mix well, and pour curry into yuzu bowls before serving. Or, serve over hot rice (sticky rice or short grain brown rice are ideal for this).

BLUEBERRY-MARINATED ROASTED TEMPEH

An improvisation that was written down -- well, sort of. You know how improvisations and memories go. A few days after making this for a dinner concert at which Michael Manring was performing, I decided to try to redo a gem of a dish. Never have repeated it the same as the fruit or berry and spices are always changing. However, this is a very wonderful start. From here, fly with it.

YIELD: 2-4 SERVINGS

Marinade:
1 tablespoon pomegranate molasses
1 tablespoon soy sauce
1/4 cup Kombu Stock (page 97)
1 tablespoon maple syrup
1/4 cup blueberries, pureed in a blender
1/4 teaspoon coriander
1/4 teaspoon cardamom

1/2 pound tempeh

Combine marinade ingredients and marinate the tempeh for 2 hours. Place tempeh with the marinade in a roasting pan. Cover tightly and roast at 425°F for 20 minutes or till marinade gets thick and glazes the tempeh.

Variation: Instead of roasting the marinated tempeh, smoke it over maple or apple or cherry wood.

Variations: Substitute the blueberries with blackberries or cherries, and omit the cardamom.

PEACH-ROASTED TEMPEH (OR APPLE OR PEAR)

Again, this recipe is merely a springboard for improvisation! The fruit and spices are always changing based on season and what we are serving it with.

YIELD: 4-8 SERVINGS

Marinade:
3 tablespoons pomegranate molasses
1 tablespoon tamarind extract
2 tablespoons red miso
1 teaspoon cumin, ground
1 teaspoon smoked paprika
1 cup stock
2 tablespoons mirin
1 teaspoon freshly cracked black pepper
1 tablespoon shoyu

1 pound tempeh
Several peaches, peeled and sliced

Combine the marinade ingredients. Place the blocks of tempeh in the marinade and let marinate for at least 4 hours, or overnight if possible. Cover the tempeh blocks with sliced, peeled peaches. Keep the tempeh in the marinade and roast at 425°F for 30 minutes, covered. Slice and serve while still warm.

Variations: Change the fruit! This works great with cherries, blackberries, tangerines, and pears in particular. Or smoke the tempeh over cherry wood. If smoking, remove the tempeh from the marinade before smoking.

TEMPEH MOLE

A huge hit whenever we prepare this.

YIELD: 4-6 SERVINGS

1 pound tempeh, cut into 3/4-inch cubes
Oil for deep-frying
Mole Sauce (page 51)

Deep-fry tempeh cubes till golden brown or steam for
20 minutes. Add to mole sauce and simmer at least 10
minutes before serving.

SPANISH BEAN SALAD

When Spain won the World Cup, we held a celebration at the underground restaurant, serving Spanish dishes named after some of the great players of that exceptional team of football improvisors. That night was dedicated particularly to Carles Puyol and Xavi Hernandes.

Use at least two kinds of beans for a variety of textures and flavors. Traditionally this is made with red kidney beans and chickpeas. Here in California we have an amazing bean farm, Rancho Gordo, which grows a large variety of heirloom beans. They are more expensive but well worth it due to their exquisite flavors and textures.

YIELD: 4-8 SERVINGS

1 cup green beans, cut into 1-inch lengths

1 quart boiling water with 1/8 teaspoon baking soda added

3 cups cooked beans

1 carrot, grated

1/2 red onion, chopped

1 clove garlic, minced

1/3 cup red wine vinegar

1/4 cup extra-virgin olive oil

1 teaspoon oregano

1 teaspoon rosemary

1 teaspoon smoked paprika

2 teaspoons sea salt

Drop the green beans in the boiling water with the baking soda added. Cook 10 seconds, drain, and rinse in cold water to stop the cooking process. Add to a bowl with the cooked beans. Combine the remaining ingredients with the beans, toss gently, and adjust the seasonings.

BLACK BEAN STEW SERVED IN DUMPLING SQUASH BOWLS

A winter favorite.

YIELD: SERVES 4-8

1 cup dried black beans, soaked overnight
1 bay leaf

2 tablespoons olive oil
1 onion, chopped
1 1/2 teaspoons sea salt
10 cloves garlic, minced
2 carrots, diced
2 jalapeños, minced
1 red pepper, chopped
1 teaspoon cumin
1 teaspoon marjoram
1 teaspoon oregano
1 teaspoon sweet paprika
1 teaspoon ancho chili powder
1 teaspoon pasilla chili powder
2 tablespoons lemon juice
1/4 cup cilantro, chopped, for garnish
3 green onions, chopped, for garnish

4-8 dumpling squash bowls (page 31)

Rinse and drain the soaked black beans. In a pot add 1 quart water, bay leaf, and the beans. Bring to a boil, cover, lower heat, and simmer 40 minutes or till beans are soft. Set aside.

In a hot saucepan, add olive oil, onion, and sea salt and sauté for 5 minutes. Add garlic, carrots, jalapeños, and red pepper and cook 5 minutes. Add all spices and cook 10 minutes. Add a little water from the bean pot if it starts to stick. Add lemon juice and adjust seasonings. Add cooked beans to the pot, remove bay leaf, and stir well. Let simmer at least 10 minutes to blend flavors. To serve, garnish with cilantro and green onions.

This stew works well alone but serve it in hot dumpling squash bowls for a special treat! The stew can also be made in advance and reheated for serving.

GARBANZO CURRY

Warming winter food.

YIELD: 4 SERVINGS

1 cup dried garbanzo beans, soaked overnight, drained, and rinsed
1 bay leaf
1 tablespoon coconut oil
1 teaspoon cumin seeds
1 teaspoon black mustard seeds
1 onion, chopped
4 cloves garlic, minced
1 tablespoon ginger, minced
1-4 green chilis, chopped
1 teaspoon coriander
1 teaspoon turmeric
1 teaspoon ground cumin
1 carrot, chopped
1 tablespoon palm sugar
1 tablespoon tamarind extract
1 cup coconut milk
1/4 cup soy sauce
1/4 cup cilantro, chopped, for garnish

In a saucepan, bring a quart of water to a boil, add the soaked/rinsed beans and bay leaf, cover, lower heat, and cook 45 minutes or till beans are tender. Remove bay leaf, drain the beans, and set the beans aside.

In a hot wok, heat up coconut oil. Add cumin seeds and mustard seeds and cook till they start to pop. Add onion, garlic, ginger, and chilis and cook 5 minutes. Add coriander, turmeric, cumin, and carrot and cook 5 more minutes. Add palm sugar and tamarind extract and mix gently. Add coconut milk and soy sauce and bring to a simmer. Do not cover!!

Add chickpeas and simmer with the rest of the ingredients for a few minutes over low heat, uncovered. Adjust seasonings with salt and tamarind if needed. Garnish with cilantro. Serve over hot basmati rice.

AZUKI BEANS WITH KABOCHA

Korean flavors; ginger and chilis to keep you warm on a cold winter evening.

YIELD: 4-6 SERVINGS

1 cup azuki beans, soaked overnight and rinsed and drained
1 quart Kombu Stock (page 97)
2 tablespoons sake
2 tablespoons mirin
2 tablespoons minced ginger
1 onion, chopped
2 cups kabocha, chopped
1/3 cup red miso

In a saucepan, bring stock to boil. Add the rest of ingredients, EXCEPT the miso.

Bring to a simmer, cover tightly, lower heat, and cook 35 minutes or till beans are tender.

Dissolve miso in 1/2 cup of the bean cooking liquid. Add to the beans. Adjust seasonings. Serve hot as a soup or a stew.

FALAFEL

A classic dish from the Middle East. Food like this crosses cultural and geographical boundaries and you can find regional variations throughout the Middle East. Loved by followers of Islam and Judaism and, well, anyone who likes the fresh taste of a delightful little ball right out of the fryer. Put a couple of hungry Palestinians in a room with a couple of hungry Israelis and put in between them some beautiful bowls of olives, hummus, falafel, lavash, and pita breads, and see the differences evaporate while the commonality of these cuisines and the delight that wonderful food produces will take over.

You will find dozens of variations on this recipe but one of the most important things about making falafel is DO NOT COOK THE BEANS! That is right, simply soak the beans and then grind them down. Do not cook them first or the texture will be shot. I know most recipes online tell you to cook the beans, but one of the problems with the internet is that rank amateurs can post incorrect information.

YIELD: ABOUT 2 DOZEN

1 pound dried garbanzos, soaked overnight, then rinsed and drained (You can mix
  garbanzos and favas if you desire. Favas are a very different taste than garbanzos.)
1/4 cup parsley leaves
1/4 cup cilantro leaves
1/4 cup fresh dill
4 green onions
4 cloves garlic
1 onion
1 teaspoon cumin
1 teaspoon coriander
1 teaspoons black pepper
1 1/2 teaspoon sea salt
1 teaspoon baking powder
Oil for deep-frying

In a food processor, grind down the beans and then add the remaining ingredients except the oil. Mix well and let sit in the fridge for 2 hours or more.

Make small, golfball-size pieces and drop in hot oil and fry till brown.

Ideally these are served with pita bread (or lavash), tahini sauce, and pickled and fresh vegetables for a truly incredible sandwich. Oh yeah, and some hot sauce!

DESSERTS

FRUIT KANTEN

Potential for improvising is enormous here! Once you understand how kanten works, you can vary the juices and fillings for an endless variety of colors and tastes.

YIELD: ABOUT 15 SERVINGS

1 cup blueberry juice
2 teaspoons kanten (agar) powder or equivalent in bar or flakes
Fresh seasonal fruit, sliced
Seasonal berries

In a saucepan, heat 2 cups water and juice. Add kanten powder and, with a whisk, constantly stir to dissolve. Bring the mixture to a boil, lower heat, and cook, stirring constantly for 3 minutes. Pour the kanten mixture into a 9-by-13-inch pan. Decorate with fresh fruit slices and berries. Let set 2 hours in the refrigerator. Serve chilled.

CABERNET KANTEN

YIELD: ABOUT 15 SERVINGS

3 cups Cabernet Sauvignon
2 teaspoons kanten (agar) powder

In a saucepan add wine and kanten. Whisk together till dissolved. Stirring often, bring to a boil, then lower heat and stir continuously at a simmer for 2 minutes. Pour into a tray and let set 2 hours in the refrigerator.

Options: Add fresh fruit to the kanten. Cherries in spring are ideal!

Vary the variety of wine. Pinots and Zinfandels can make a great kanten!

TRUFFLES

YIELD: ABOUT 3 DOZEN TRUFFLES

2 cups raw cashews
1 cup maple syrup
1 tablespoon soy sauce (high-quality tamari is preferable)
1 cup cocoa powder

In a food processor, add cashews and process them down to a very smooth nut butter. Once it is smooth, add maple syrup and blend very well, till homogenized. Add soy sauce and cocoa powder and process till smooth and combined. Place the mixture in a bowl, cover, and refrigerate at least 2 hours.

Shape into small balls. I like to use a small ice cream scoop for these.

Roll the truffles in any of the following: green tea powder, cocoa powder, cocoa powder with any spices added to it.

You can also fill the truffles with pieces of nuts, cocoa nibs, fruit, dried fruit and/or spices.

This same mixture can make an excellent icing for cakes! When using as an icing, do NOT refrigerate!

Variation: Sichuan Peppercorn/Yuzu Truffles

Koto player Shoko Hikage was a little concerned after trying these, as she whispered to me, "My tongue is numb, what did you put in these?"

The combination of Sichuan peppercorns and yuzu is a personal favorite.

Stuff each truffle with 1 sichuan peppercorn and some yuzu zest!

RUGELACH

A childhood favorite! My Aunt Rose's kitchen was always a joyful place to visit as she always had amazing food coming out of her oven. Rugelach was one of her specialties. The love of making rugelach was transmitted from Aunt Rose to my sister Barbie who actually managed to surpass Aunt Rose as the supreme master rugelach maker of our family. Both of them are gone, sadly, and this veganized version of Aunt Rose's recipe hopefully honors these two amazing women from my family! Rugelach is made with a cream cheese dough, so I use my cashew chèvre as a replacement in these delightful cookies.

YIELD: ABOUT 3 DOZEN

Dough:
3/4 cup grapeseed oil
1/2 cup Cashew Chèvre (page 43)
1 tablespoon lemon juice
1/3 cup maple syrup
1/2 teaspoon sea salt
2 cups flour

Filling:
1/3 cups dried fruit, chopped (see note)
1 cup chopped nuts (see note)
1/3 cup maple syrup
1/2 teaspoon cinnamon
1/4 teaspoon sea salt

Mix oil, cashew chèvre, lemon juice, potato starch, maple syrup, and salt very well! Add the flour, gently, bringing the dough together. Do NOT mix well and do not try to homogenize the dough. As always, when working with wheat flour for desserts, we want to avoid creating glutens, thus we must be very delicate with mixing. Form a ball, wrap tightly, and refrigerate for 1 hour.

Preheat oven to 375°F.

Mix the filling ingredients well. Set aside.

Roll out the dough on a large table or board till 1/4 inch thin. Spread filling on one end. Roll up into a log in the same fashion you would roll a cinnamon roll. Cut into cookies, each 2 inches in length. Place cookies 1 inch apart on an oiled baking sheet. Bake on middle oven rack for 18 minutes or till lightly browned. Remove to a rack to cool.

Note: Raisins are the dried fruit traditionally used here; dried cranberries or dried currants work very nicely as well. Walnuts are the traditional nut; pecans are a wonderful substitute.

BROWNIES

YIELD: 1 9-BY-13-INCH PAN, ABOUT 15 SERVINGS

Wet mix:
1 cup grapeseed oil
1 cup maple syrup
1/2 cup soy milk (see note)
1/4 cup Cashew Chèvre (page 43)

Dry mix:
2 cups white flour
1 cup cocoa
3/4 cup palm sugar
2 teaspoons baking powder
1 teaspoon sea salt
1 cup chopped pecans
1 cup chocolate chips

Preheat oven to 350°F. In one bowl, whisk together the wet ingredients. In another bowl whisk together the dry ingredients. Add wet to dry, stirring gently. Do NOT overmix or the results will be rubbery.

Pour batter into an oiled 9-by-13-inch pan. Bake on the middle oven rack for 30 minutes or till a toothpick inserted in the center comes out clean.

Note: Only use soy milk made of 2 ingredients: organic soybeans and water. Any additives (sugars, gums, stabilizers) will simply destroy the results you are seeking.

CARROT-OAT COOKIES

Food, for most of us, inevitably becomes tied with memories. This recipe is dedicated to the memory of Paul Decker! I used to see Paul at many concerts of mine and others, usually accompanied by his girlfriend, flute player Polly Moller. He was quite shy and did not say much. Then when I started to offer cooking classes, Paul began attending. His shyness went away in small groups, especially with a lot of food in front of him. He was quite passionate about food and cooking and he and Polly would often email me about his experiments with recipes he was learning from me. Paul grew up in Mississippi and when I would say "pecan" with my New York accent, he would laugh and always critique it and say it in the Southern manner.

Paul tragically took his own life, several years ago. I always think of him when I bake these cookies, which were one of his favorites, and I always laugh to myself when I say "pecan," thinking of him.

YIELD: ABOUT 3 DOZEN COOKIES

Wet mix:
1/2 cup maple syrup
1/2 cup grapeseed oil
1 teaspoon vanilla extract

Dry mix:
1 cup oats
1 cup flour
1 teaspoon cinnamon
1 teaspoon baking powder
1/2 teaspoon baking soda
1/4 teaspoon salt

1 cup grated carrots
1/2 cup chopped pecans
1/2 cup dried cherries (see note)

In one bowl, combine wet ingredients. In another bowl, combine the dry ingredients. Add wet mix to dry mix and combine gently. Add carrots, nuts, and dried fruit to this mix and blend gently. Do NOT overmix or the cookies will be rubbery.

These cookies only bake well if they are small. Drop cookie batter in teaspoonfuls onto an oiled baking sheet. Bake on the middle oven rack for 10 minutes. Be careful not to overbake as they burn easily after they are done.

Note: Dried cherries can be replaced by currants, raisins, dried blueberries, or dried cranberries. Or a combination!

CHOCOLATE CHIP COOKIES

Cori came up with this recipe in our kitchen!

YIELD: ABOUT 3 DOZEN COOKIES

Wet mix:
2/3 cup maple syrup
1 tablespoon vanilla extract
1 teaspoon blackstrap molasses
1/3 cup Cashew Chèvre (page 43)
1/2 cup oil

Dry mix:
2 cups flour
4 teaspoons cocoa
1 teaspoon baking soda
2 teaspoons baking powder
1/2 teaspoon sea salt
1/2 cup palm sugar
1 teaspoon cinnamon

2/3 cup chocolate chips
2/3 cup chopped nuts

Preheat oven to 350°F.

Combine wet ingredients in one bowl. Mix dry ingredients in another bowl. Add wet to dry. Mix gently. Fold in chocolate chips and nuts. Using a small ice cream scoop, shape cookies and place on an oiled baking sheet, about 1 inch apart.

Bake on middle oven rack for 11 minutes, until done.

CHOCOLATE PISTACHIO CAKE

Another of Cori's creations in our kitchen!

YIELD: 1 9-INCH CAKE

Dry mix:
1 cup flour
1 cup cocoa
2 teaspoons baking powder
1 teaspoon baking soda
1/2 teaspoon sea salt

Wet mix:
1/2 cup pistachios
1/4 cup blueberries, optional
1/2 cup maple syrup
1 cup soy milk (see note)
1/2 cup grapeseed oil
2 teaspoons vanilla extract
1 teaspoon yuzu juice or cider vinegar

Preheat oven to 350°F.

Whisk together the dry ingredients in a bowl. Separately, place the wet ingredients into a blender and puree for 2 minutes. Pour the wet mix over the dry mix and gently combine, leaving some lumps. Pour into an oiled 9-inch cake pan.

Bake on middle oven rack for 25 minutes until done. Test for doneness by inserting a toothpick in the center of the cake. If it comes out clean, it's done.

This cake is excellent covered in truffle frosting (page 157). Cover the frosting with toasted pistachios and raw berries.

Note: Only use soy milk made of 2 ingredients: organic soybeans and water. Any additives (sugars, gums, stabilizers) will simply destroy the results you are seeking.

MATCHA YUZU CAKE

Another original, obviously Japanese-inspired recipe using two of my favorite ingredients, matcha and yuzu! The bittersweet flavor of the tea along with the tart yuzu flavor is a delightful combination! And who does not love green cake?

YIELD: ONE 8-INCH ROUND CAKE

Dry mix:

2 cups white flour

1 teaspoon baking powder

1/2 teaspoon baking soda

1 tablespoon matcha

1/4 teaspoon sea salt

Wet mix:

1/3 cup grapeseed oil

3/4 cup maple syrup

1 cup soy milk (see note)

2 tablespoon yuzu juice

1 teaspoon vanilla extract

Preheat oven to 350°F. In a bowl combine the dry ingredients. In a separate bowl, combine the wet ingredients. Add wet to dry and mix very gently. Do not overmix! Pour into an oiled 8-inch round cake pan.

Bake for 45 minutes or till a toothpick inserted into the center of the cake comes out clean.

Note: Only use soy milk made of 2 ingredients: organic soybeans and water. Any additives (sugars, gums, stabilizers) will simply destroy the results you are seeking.

CORN SORBET

Two pieces of equipment are needed to make the sorbet and ice cream recipes: a high-speed blender and an ice cream freezer.

YIELD: 1 QUART

4 ears corn
1/4 teaspoon sea salt
1/2 cup maple syrup
1/2 cup raw cashews
2 teaspoons vanilla extract

Add corn and salt to a roasting pan, rubbing salt into the corn. Cover tightly and roast at 425°F for 35 minutes or till the corn starts to lightly brown. The caramelizing is integral to get a lot of sweetness out of the corn. Cool ears of corn until you can handle them, and then slice kernels off the cob with a large knife.

Place roasted corn, maple syrup, cashews, and 1 cup water in a high-speed blender and process 5 minutes or till very smooth. Add vanilla and an additional 1 cup water and mix well. Freeze in an ice cream freezer according to the manufacturer's instructions.

PEACH-WALNUT SORBET

YIELD: 1 QUART

1/2 cup cashews
1 cup raw walnuts
1/2 cup maple syrup
4 very ripe peaches, chopped (remove pit!)
1 teaspoon rosewater
1 teaspoon vanilla extract
A dash of salt

In a high-speed blender, place cashews, walnuts, 1 cup water and maple syrup. Process on high speed for 5 minutes till very smooth. Add peaches, rosewater, vanilla, and salt and blend to mix. Freeze in an ice cream freezer according to the manufacturer's instructions.

DOUBLE CHOCOLATE ICE CREAM

YIELD: 1 QUART

1 cup raw cashews
1/2 cup maple syrup
3 cups soy milk (see note)
A dash of salt
1/2 cup cocoa powder
3/4 cup chocolate chips

In a high-speed blender, place cashews, maple syrup, 1 cup soy milk, salt, and cocoa powder. Process on high for 5 minutes or till very smooth. Add remaining 2 cups soy milk and blend well. Stir in chocolate chips. Freeze in an ice cream freezer according to the manufacturer's instructions.

Optional: Add 1/2 cup toasted nuts when you stir in the chocolate chips.

Note: Only use soy milk made of 2 ingredients: organic soybeans and water. Any additives (sugars, gums, stabilizers) will simply destroy the results you are seeking.

PEACH-PECAN BOURBON ICE CREAM

YIELD: 1 QUART

1/2 cup raw cashews
1 cup raw pecans
1/2 cup maple syrup
A dash of salt
3 cups peaches, chopped, pits discarded
1-2 tablespoons bourbon

In a high-speed blender, place cashews, pecans, maple syrup, salt, and 1 cup water. Process 5 minutes or till very smooth. Add the rest of the ingredients and blend for 30 seconds. Freeze in an ice cream freezer according to the manufacturer's instructions.

BLUEBERRY SORBET

YIELD: 1 QUART

1 cup raw cashews
1/2 cup maple syrup
3 cups blueberries
2 teaspoons vanilla extract
1/2 vanilla bean, split and seeded (use the seeds; discard the woody pod or use it in a different recipe)
A dash of salt

In a high-speed blender, add cashews, 1 cup water and maple syrup. Process 5 minutes or till very smooth. Add the rest of the ingredients to the blender and process again, till smooth, about 30 seconds. Freeze in an ice cream freezer according to the manufacturer's instructions.

CHERRY-PISTACHIO SORBET

YIELD: 1 QUART

1 cup raw pistachios
1/2 cup maple syrup
3 cups pitted cherries
2 teaspoons vanilla extract

In a high-speed blender, add pistachios, 1 cup water, and maple syrup and process on high speed for 5 minutes or till very smooth. Add the rest of the ingredients and process for 30 seconds. Freeze in an ice cream freezer according to the manufacturer's instructions.

BANANA-WALNUT CHOCOLATE CHIP SORBET

YIELD: 1 QUART

3 very ripe bananas
1/2 cup maple syrup
1 cup raw walnuts
2 tablespoons dark rum
A dash of salt
1/2 cup chocolate chips
1/3 cup toasted chopped walnuts

In a high-speed blender, add bananas, maple syrup, walnuts, and 1 cup water and process on high for 3 minutes or till very smooth. Add rum, salt, and an additonal 1 cup water and process 30 seconds. Stir in chocolate chips and toasted walnuts. Freeze in an ice cream freezer according to the manufacturer's instructions.

YUZU SORBET

YIELD: 1 QUART

1 cup yuzu juice
1/2 cup maple syrup

Combine the ingredients and 3 cups water in a blender. Freeze in an ice cream freezer according to the manufacturer's instructions.

CRANBERRY-YUZU WALNUT ICE CREAM

YIELD: 1 QUART

1 cup raw walnuts
1/2 cup raw cashews
1/2 cup maple syrup
1 cup raw cranberries
Juice and zest of 1 yuzu
1 teaspoon vanilla extract

In a high-speed blender place walnuts, cashews, maple syrup, and 2 cups water and process on high for 5 minutes or till very smooth. Add the rest of the ingredients and process 30 seconds. Freeze in an ice cream freezer according to the manufacturer's instructions.

ROSEWATER-SAFFRON ICE CREAM

This Persian treat highlights the beautiful color, taste, and aroma of saffron.

YIELD: 1 QUART

3 cups soy milk (see note)
1/2 cup maple syrup
1 cup raw cashews
1 tablespoon rosewater
.25 grams saffron

In a high-speed blender, place 1 cup soy milk, maple syrup, and cashews and process on high speed for 5 minutes, till very smooth. Add the rest of the ingredients and process for 30 seconds. Freeze in an ice cream freezer according to the manufacturer's instructions.

Note: Only use soy milk made of 2 ingredients: organic soybeans and water. Any additives (sugars, gums, stabilizers) will simply destroy the results you are seeking.

WATERMELON SORBET

YIELD: 1 QUART

4 cups cubed watermelon
1 tablespoon lemon juice

Puree watermelon in a high-speed blender and add lemon juice. Freeze in an ice cream freezer according to the manufacturer's instructions.

INDEX

DIPS
Beet-Nut Pâté 64
Black Bean Puree 73
Cashew Chèvre 43
Guacamole 73
Hummus 65
Mango Salsa 72
Smoked Eggplant Spread 70

EGGPLANT
Rollatini 123
Smoked Eggplant Spread 70
Tempeh with Sour Yuzu Curry 146

FERMENTED BEAN CURD
Corn Fritters 66
Definition 26
Green Papaya Salad 57
Ong Choy with Garlic and
    Fermented Bean Curd 119
Peanut Sauce 34
Pumpkin Fritters 67
Tempeh Char Siu 140
Yuzu Curry Paste 124

FERMENTED BLACK BEANS
Definition 25
Gai Lan with Garlic and Ginger 121
Tofu with Black Bean Sauce 133

JAPANESE DISHES
Amazake 41
Azuki Beans with Kabocha 153
Fruit Kanten 156
Peach Mustard 47
Mirin 42
Noodle Soup 111
Ramen 86
Smoked Tofu Yuba Wraps with Mustard 58
Soba 87
Tempeh Dengaku 144
Tempeh with Yuzu Curry 146
Tempeh Terriyaki 141
Yuzu Bowls 30
Yuzu Curry Paste 124

JEWISH DISHES
Knishes 60
Latkes 115
Rugelach 158

LEMONGRASS
Corn Fritters 66
Lemongrass Coconut Soup 110
Lemongrass Tempeh 145
Peanut Sauce 34
Pumpkin Fritters 67
Southeast Asian Stock 98
Tempeh Larb 142
Thai Style Noodle Soup 113
Yuzu Curry Paste 124

MAKRUT LIME LEAVES
Definition 25
Corn Fritters 66
Pumpkin Fritters 67
Southeast Asian Stock 98
Lemongrass Coconut Soup
    with Glass Noodles 110
Thai Noodle Soup 113

MUSTARD
Blueberry Mustard 52
Cherry Mustard 52
Chinese Style Mustard 52
Peach Mustard 47
Smoked Yuba Wraps 58
Steamed Dumplings filled with
    Tempeh Char Siu 93
Stout Mustard 47
Tea Smoked Tofu 130